FIFTH EDITION

READY TO WRITE 2

PERFECTING PARAGRAPHS

KAREN BLANCHARD • CHRISTINE ROOT

This book is dedicated to the memory of our parents, Betty and Herbert Lourie and Charlotte and Stanley Baker, who taught us to love learning and to understand the power and magic of the written word.

Ready to Write 2: Perfecting Paragraphs
Fifth Edition

Pearson Education, 221 River Street, Hoboken, NJ 07030

Acknowledgments: We are grateful to several people whose advice and contributions enriched this book. Thank you to Lynn Whitnall, Andrea J. Brooks, Daniel L. Blanchard, and Robby Steinberg. We also appreciate the hard work of Amy McCormick and Penny Laporte for their steadfast support of us and our work over the course of the five editions of Ready to Write 2!

Staff credits: The people who made up the *Ready to Write* team, representing editorial, production, design, and manufacturing, are Pietro Alongi, Tracey Cataldo, Rosa Chapinal, Aerin Csigay, Mindy DePalma, Warren Fischbach, Pam Fishman, Leslie Johnson, Niki Lee, Amy McCormick, Robert Ruvo, and Kristina Skof.
Development Editor: Penny Laporte
Cover image: Evgeny Karandaev / Shutterstock
Text composition: ElectraGraphics, Inc.
Text font: Formata Light

Library of Congress Cataloging-in-Publication Data
A catalog record for the print edition is available from the Library of Congress.
ISBN-10: 0-13-439932-3   ISBN-13: 978-0-13-439932-4

Printed in the United States of America
5   17

Contents

Scope and Sequence

Chapter	Grammar for Writing	Writer's Tips	Writing Activities
1 **GETTING ORGANIZED** **Learning Outcome:** Organize items on a list into groups	• Capitalization and punctuation	• Organizing information into groups • Identifying irrelevant information	• Writing and organizing lists • Organizing items into groups
2 **UNDERSTANDING PARAGRAPHS** **Learning Outcome:** Write a well-organized paragraph with a topic sentence, supporting sentences, and a concluding sentence	• Compound sentences	• Paragraph form • Topic sentence • Paragraph unity	• Identifying parts of a paragraph • Writing topic, supporting, and concluding sentences • Using topic sentences as prompts for paragraphs • Following steps to write well-organized paragraphs
3 **ORGANIZING INFORMATION BY TIME ORDER** **Learning Outcome:** Write a paragraph organized by time order	• Prepositions of time • Complex sentences with *before* and *after*	• Signal words • Writing titles for paragraphs	• Writing an email using prepositions of time • Writing paragraphs in chronological order prompted by schedules, lists, and time lines • Writing biographical paragraphs **WORD BANKS** Signal words that show time order Other signals of time order
4 **ORGANIZING INFORMATION BY ORDER OF IMPORTANCE** **Learning Outcome:** Write a paragraph listing the supporting ideas in order of importance	• Comma splices	• Gerunds in topic sentences • Adding new ideas	• Writing topic sentences for order of importance paragraphs • Writing and ordering supporting points • Writing paragraphs organized by order of importance • Writing equal-order paragraphs **WORD BANK** Order of importance signal words

Chapter	Grammar for Writing	Writer's Tips	Writing Activities
5 **ORGANIZING INFORMATION BY SPATIAL ORDER** **Learning Outcome:** Write a paragraph describing a place using spatial order	• Prepositions of place	• Organizing details	• Writing topic sentences for spatial order paragraphs • Organizing details in spatial order • Writing descriptive paragraphs using spatial order **WORD BANK** Prepositions of place
6 **UNDERSTANDING THE WRITING PROCESS** **Learning Outcome:** Write a paragraph using the three steps of the writing process	• Sentence fragments	• Writing the first draft	• Recognizing and using the steps of the writing process • Brainstorming, clustering, listing • Organizing ideas into lists and outlines • Revising and editing paragraphs
7 **SUPPORTING THE MAIN IDEA** **Learning Outcome:** Write a paragraph using charts, graphs, and quotes to support the main idea	• Introducing examples: Using *for example, for instance, such as* • Punctuating quotes	• Providing support	• Using the writing process • Writing paragraphs with supporting examples, personal experiences, facts, statistics, information from graphs and charts, and quotes **WORD BANKS** Verbs that describe change Adjectives and adverbs describing degree of change Verbs that introduce quotes
8 **EXPLAINING A PROCESS** **Learning Outcome:** Write a paragraph describing the steps in a process	• Imperative sentences	• Time order signal words	• Using the writing process • Writing topic sentences for process paragraphs • Ordering sentences in process paragraphs • Writing process paragraphs **WORD BANK** Direction signal words

Chapter	Grammar for Writing	Writer's Tips	Writing Activities
9 **WRITING DESCRIPTIONS** **Learning Outcome:** Write a paragraph using descriptive details about a person, place or thing	• Order of adjectives	• Sensory words • Using adjectives	• Using the writing process • Writing topic sentences for descriptive paragraphs • Writing details in descriptive paragraphs • Writing descriptive paragraphs about people, places, and objects **WORD BANKS** Words to describe people Common sensory words Words for describing places
10 **EXPRESSING YOUR OPINION** **Learning Outcome:** Write a paragraph that expresses your opinion on a number of topics	• Run-on sentences	• Using reasons	• Using the writing process • Writing topic sentences for opinion paragraphs • Writing supporting details for opinion paragraphs • Writing opinion paragraphs
11 **COMPARING AND CONTRASTING** **Learning Outcome:** Write a paragraph comparing or contrasting two people, experiences, or things	• Sentence patterns of comparison • Comparative adjectives	• Compare and contrast	• Using the writing process • Writing topic sentences for comparison and contrast paragraphs • Writing paragraphs of comparison and contrast

Chapter	Grammar for Writing	Writer's Tips	Writing Activities
12 **ANALYZING CAUSES AND EFFECTS** **Learning Outcome:** Write a paragraph describing the causes or effects of an event	• Complex sentences with *because* and *since*	• Paragraph unity	• Using the writing process • Writing topic sentences for cause and effect paragraphs • Writing cause and effect paragraphs
13 **WRITING SUMMARIES AND ANSWERING TEST QUESTIONS** **Learning Outcome:** Write a paragraph that summarizes an article or a story	• Agreement of subjects and verbs • Verb and pronoun agreement	• Subject/verb agreement • Steps in writing a summary • Answering test questions	• Using the writing process • Identifying main ideas and details • Writing summaries • Writing answers to test questions
14 **WRITING PERSONAL LETTERS AND BUSINESS LETTERS** **Learning Outcome:** Write personal and business letters	• Capitalization and punctuation in letters	• Personal letters • Addressing envelopes • Business letters	• Writing personal letters • Writing business letters • Writing letters of complaint and praise

Introduction

Ready to Write 2 is a high-beginning/low-intermediate writing skills textbook for students of English as a Second Language who have mastered the basics of both written and spoken English. *Ready to Write 2* is designed to acquaint students with the skills required for good writing and help them become comfortable, confident, and independent writers in English.

The *Ready to Write series* came about because of our threefold conviction that

- students learn to write well and achieve a more complete English proficiency by learning and practicing writing skills simultaneously with other English language skills they are learning;

- students are interested in and capable of writing expressively in English—however basic the language—on a variety of provocative and sophisticated topics if they are supplied with the basic vocabulary and organizational tools;

- students need to be explicitly taught that different languages organize information differently, and they need to be shown how to organize information correctly in English.

Approach

Based on these assumptions, *Ready to Write 2* is intended to provide students with a wide variety of stimulating writing topics and activities that go beyond sentence manipulation drills. Students are thereby encouraged to bring their own ideas and talents to the writing process. With a focus on the process of writing paragraphs, students learn, step-by-step, the organizational principles that will help them express themselves effectively in English. They also learn to apply these principles to a variety of rhetorical formats.

As in *Ready to Write 1* and *Ready to Write 3,* the activities are designed to encourage students to think independently and to provide them with many opportunities for sharing ideas with their classmates, thus creating a more dynamic learning environment. To this end, collaborative writing and peer feedback activities are included in all the chapters. In addition, great care has been taken to maintain an appropriate level of vocabulary and complexity of sentence structure for high-beginning and low-intermediate students so that the explanations, directions, and readings are easily accessible.

The Fifth Edition

While much has been updated and expanded in this Fifth Edition of *Ready to Write 2,* what has not changed is the successful, basic approach that has made the series so popular all these years.

Two popular features from the previous editions—*You Be the Editor* and *On Your Own*—continue to appear regularly in this edition. *You Be the Editor* provides practice in error correction and proofreading in order to help students monitor their own errors. (An Answer Key for this section appears at the end of the book.) *On Your Own* provides students with further individual practice in the paragraph-writing skills they have learned.

The fifth edition of *Ready to Write 2* includes these important new and expanded features:

- learning outcomes at the beginning of each chapter to focus students on the chapter's goals
- an engaging four-color design to help learners' visual literacy and highlight key features
- updated, expanded, and reinforced explanations and model paragraphs
- extensive targeted grammar practice to help students become effective writers
- enhanced and increased sentence and writing process tasks to encourage experimentation, creativity, and bolster writing practice and accuracy
- *Essential Online Resources* with answer keys, as well as additional grammar and writing activities.

OVERVIEW OF THE CHAPTERS

Learning Outcomes: Each chapter begins with objectives so students can see the intended goals of a chapter and what their learning experience will be. The learning outcomes are brief, written statements that help students see the knowledge, skills, and habits of work that they are expected to acquire by the end of the chapter.

Grammar for Writing: Each chapter focuses on one or two specific grammar points along with helpful charts, clear explanations, and attendant practice. By practicing new grammar points in the context of their writing, students boost their writing accuracy and learn to vary their sentence types.

The Steps of the Writing Process: Each chapter provides guided instruction in the steps that are integral to good writing i.e. prewriting, writing, and revising. Revising checklists are provided for students to use to improve their paragraphs and write their final draft.

Writer's Tips: This feature provides helpful information on how to write and refine paragraphs. These tips include choosing a topic and working toward unity, accuracy and coherence.

On Your Own: Coming toward the end of most chapters, these activities provide students with yet another opportunity to write on a topic of their own choosing from among several suggested prompts. After they write a paragraph, students are instructed to use the revising checklist to improve their paragraphs, thereby practicing independent writing and revising.

You Be the Editor: This self-correcting exercise near the end of each chapter is intended to give students the opportunity to look for and correct the most common grammar mistakes made by high beginning students as they learn to write in English. Each paragraph has a stated number of mistakes for students to look for. The answers for each chapter appear in the back of the book. Students can use the answers to check their own work and become independent and confident writers.

We hope that you enjoy working through these activities with your students. At any level, they are definitely *ready to write*.
—*KLB and CBR*

CHAPTER 1 Getting Organized

Writing can be difficult in your own language. In a new language, writing can be even more difficult. The good news is that writing involves skills that you can learn, practice, and master. As you work through this book, you will learn and practice the skills you need to become a good writer in English.

Copyright 2004 by Randy Glasbergen.
www.glasbergen.com

**"I am not disorganized—I know *exactly* where everything is!
The newer stuff is on top and the older stuff is on the bottom."**

THE KEY TO GOOD WRITING

Organization is the key to good writing. Different languages organize ideas differently. In this chapter, you will begin to learn how to organize information in English so that you can write effective paragraphs.

Organizing Information into Groups

One way to organize information is to group similar ideas together. Look at the following list of places.

- South America
- New York City
- Italy
- Korea
- Europe

- Istanbul
- Asia
- Tokyo
- Mexico

You can organize this list by dividing it into three groups. Notice that each group has something in common.

A	B	C
South America	Italy	New York City
Asia	Korea	Istanbul
Europe	Mexico	Tokyo

Work with a partner. Talk about the groups in the lists. Answer these questions.

1. What do all the places in group A have in common?

   They are continents. _____

2. What do all the places in group B have in common?

   _____

3. What do all the places in group C have in common?

   _____

Organizing Lists

You can give each group a name. The name is the topic of the list.

A **Continents**	B **Countries**	C **Cities**
South America	Italy	New York City
Asia	Korea	Istanbul
Europe	Mexico	Tokyo

 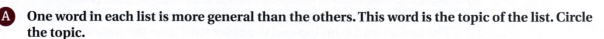 **PRACTICE** **A** **One word in each list is more general than the others. This word is the topic of the list. Circle the topic.**

1. chair	3. mail	5. waterfall
table	postcard	mountain
desk	letter	lake
(furniture)	bill	valley
sofa	package	scenery

2. necklace	4. suitcase	6. pepper
ring	duffle bag	salt
jewelry	luggage	cumin
earrings	garment bag	spices
watch	cosmetics case	paprika

B Write a topic for each list on the line. Use a dictionary if necessary.

1. _____Cars_____
convertibles
sedans
station wagons
sports cars

2. _____
engineer
teacher
lawyer
dentist

3. _____
Earth
Jupiter
Mars
Venus

4. _____
Atlantic
Pacific
Indian
Arctic

5. _____
earthquake
flood
tornado
avalanche

6. _____
gold
silver
iron
copper

7. _____
pediatrician
surgeon
cardiologist
internist

8. _____
make the beds
dust the furniture
vacuum the carpets
clean the bathroom

9. _____
love
hate
anger
joy

C Divide the words in each list into three groups. Put similar ideas together and write a topic for each group.

1. Sunday   winter
   January   spring
   February   Friday
   summer   December
   Tuesday

	A	**B**	**C**
Topic:	Days		
	Sunday		
	Tuesday		
	Friday		

2. jet   truck

bus   helicopter

boat   submarine

car   ship

airplane

A	B	C
Topic: _____	**Topic:** _____	**Topic:** _____
_____	_____	_____
_____	_____	_____
_____	_____	_____

3. ring   glasses

hat   mittens

shoes   boots

socks   headband

gloves

A	B	C
Topic: _____	**Topic:** _____	**Topic:** _____
_____	_____	_____
_____	_____	_____
_____	_____	_____

4. red   medium

small   purple

triangle   circle

square   green

large

A	B	C
Topic: _____	**Topic:** _____	**Topic:** _____
_____	_____	_____
_____	_____	_____
_____	_____	_____

Choosing a Way to Organize

Often there is more than one way to organize things into groups. For example, cars can be grouped in several ways.

Topic: Cars	**Topic:** Cars	**Topic:** Cars
Size	*Cost*	*Age*
full-size	cars that cost less than $15,000	new cars
mid-size	cars that cost between $15,000 and $25,000	used cars
compact	cars that cost more than $25,000	
subcompact		

PRACTICE **A** **Work with a partner and complete the following tasks.**

1. Think of at least two ways to organize different sports. Then list the sports for each category.

   Topic: Kinds of sports   **Topic:** Kinds of sports

   _____   _____

   _____   _____

   _____   _____

   _____   _____

2. Think of at least two ways to organize types of food. Then list the foods for each category.

   Topic: Kinds of food   **Topic:** Kinds of food

   _____   _____

   _____   _____

   _____   _____

   _____   _____

B **Make a list of all the people in your class. Organize the list by dividing the people into groups. Think of several ways to do this and write them below. Remember that all members of a group should have something in common.**

1. *Divide the students into two groups: males and females* _____

2. _____

3. _____

4. _____

5. _____

IDENTIFYING IRRELEVANT INFORMATION

All of the items in a group should have something in common. They should also relate to the topic of the group. When an item does not relate to the other items in a group, it does not belong in that group. An item that does not belong is called *irrelevant*.

PRACTICE **A** Cross out the item in each group that does not belong.

1.   **2**   **4**   **6**   ~~**5**~~

2.   ○   ∫   □   △

3.   (shapes)

4.   (rectangles with dots)

5.   =   ✕   +   ✕

6.   **30**   **25**   **28**   **15**

B Cross out the word in each group that does not belong. Then write a topic for each list.

1. _Eating Utensils_
   fork
   ~~oven~~
   spoon
   chopsticks

2. _____
   Pennsylvania
   Denver
   Florida
   California

3. _____
   noun
   comma
   verb
   adjective

4. _____
   Spanish
   Turkish
   Chinese
   Modern

5. _____
   physics
   swimming
   biology
   chemistry

6. _____
   saxophone
   piano
   engine
   drums

7. _____
   computer
   cell phone
   scanner
   washing machine

8. _____
   happy
   windy
   sad
   angry

C Cross out the sentence in each group that does not belong.

1. **Topic:** It is interesting to visit foreign countries.

    a. You can meet new people.

    b. You can eat different kinds of food.

    c. ~~It is expensive. You can spend too much money.~~

    d. You can see the way other people live.

    e. You can learn about other cultures.

2. **Topic:** Seattle is a great place to live if you like the outdoors.

    a. The weather is usually warm and pleasant.

    b. The roads are crowded and there is always a lot of traffic.

    c. You can ride a bicycle, go running, or take a walk almost any day of the year.

    d. You can go rock climbing or hiking in the nearby Cascade and Olympic Mountains.

    e. The Pacific Ocean is very close, so it is easy to go fishing, surfing, and swimming.

3. **Topic:** Small cars are becoming more popular.

    a. They are more economical.

    b. Small cars use less gas than bigger cars.

    c. They are easier to park.

    d. Some small cars are uncomfortable.

    e. Small cars are better for the environment.

4. **Topic:** Different people spend their free time in different ways.

    a. Some people spend their free time reading or watching TV.

    b. The price of movies has increased recently.

    c. Other people like to go shopping if they have some free time.

    d. Many people enjoy playing sports or watching their favorite team play.

    e. Some people like to visit their friends in their free time.

5. **Topic:** Nursing is an excellent career choice for some people.

    a. It offers a rewarding opportunity to help other people.

    b. Nurses can find interesting jobs in all areas of health care.

    c. Nurses earn a good salary and have great benefits.

    d. Some universities do not have nursing programs.

    e. Nurses often have flexible work schedules.

6. **Topic:** The new Lewis Convention Center is a great addition to our city.

   a. It creates new jobs.

   b. It brings tourists to our city.

   c. The convention center schedules interesting exhibits.

   d. The building is architecturally pleasing.

   e. There isn't enough parking at the convention center.

GRAMMAR FOR WRITING: Capitalization and Punctuation

Like most other languages, English has certain rules for capitalization and punctuation. Learning these rules will improve your writing.

Study the rules for capitalization and punctuation and read the example sentences.

RULES	EXAMPLES
Begin the first word of every sentence with a **capital letter** and end it with a **period**, **exclamation point**, or **question mark**.	**P**eople around the world drink tea**.** **L**ook at that beautiful car**!** **W**ho won the race**?**
Always capitalize the pronoun *I*.	Christine and **I** wrote this book.
Capitalize all proper nouns including • names and titles • names of places (cities, streets, countries, etc.) • names of languages, religions, and nationalities.	My name is **Dr. C**arol **W**olf. I live at 515 **P**rospect **A**venue in **T**oronto, **C**anada. My friend speaks **J**apanese fluently.
Capitalize days of the week, holidays, and months of the year, but do not capitalize the names of seasons.	My favorite holiday, **H**alloween, is next **T**uesday. I plant flowers every **s**pring and **s**ummer.
Capitalize the first word of a quote.	The teacher said, "**P**lease open your books."

PRACTICE **A** **Add the correct punctuation to the sentences.**

1. What time does the class begin

2. Please don't touch that

3. I have to do the laundry on Saturday

4. We are going to buy a new car this weekend

5. Who is your roommate

6. Be careful

B Add capital letters where necessary.

1. i plan to visit jason on monday after work.

2. your appointment is at 2:30 wednesday afternoon.

3. we are having dinner at mr. and mrs. root's house for thanksgiving.

4. my sister and i are learning korean.

5. the professor said, "your essay is due on friday."

6. they are planning a trip to toronto, canada.

C Add capital letters and punctuation to the sentences.

1. engineering is a good career choice for some people

2. my sister and i love japanese food

3. who is your favorite movie star

4. the meeting is scheduled for monday, april 25

5. i made an appointment with dr. brody for friday morning

6. do you know anyone who speaks turkish

7. matt and i will meet you on the corner of locust street and second avenue

8 mr. jones said, "the train to burlington, vermont, is running thirty minutes late."

YOU BE THE EDITOR

Read the paragraph. It contains ten errors in capitalization and punctuation. Correct the mistakes. Copy the corrected paragraph on a separate piece of paper.

A Smart Man

Many of the stories in my country, turkey, are about a clever man named nasreddin. In one story, nasreddin is walking through the marketplace when an angry shopkeeper stops him The shopkeeper yells at nasreddin for not paying the seventy-five piasters he owes him. But the clever Nasreddin says, "you know that i plan to pay you thirty-five piasters tomorrow, and next tuesday another thirty-five. that means i owe you only five piasters. You should be ashamed for yelling at me so loudly for a debt of only five piasters!" I laugh every time I think of that story.

ON YOUR OWN

Complete the following activity.

1. Choose one of the following topics and make a list.
   - things you have to do this weekend
   - places you want to visit
   - purchases you have made in the last month

2. Organize the items on your list into groups.

3. Give each group a name.

2 Understanding Paragraphs

LEARNING OUTCOME **Paragraph Writing:** Write a well-organized paragraph with a topic sentence, supporting sentences, and a concluding sentence

Most English writing is organized into paragraphs. A paragraph is a group of related sentences. Like the items on the lists in Chapter 1, the sentences in a paragraph should all have something in common. They should all relate to the topic.

IDENTIFYING PARTS OF PARAGRAPHS

Most paragraphs follow a certain format. They have three basic parts. A good paragraph usually begins with a sentence that states the main idea of the whole paragraph. This sentence is called the *topic sentence*. The next group of sentences in the paragraph explains the main idea. They add details and give support. These sentences are called *supporting sentences*. Some paragraphs end with a *concluding sentence*. This sentence restates the main idea.

Read the model paragraph. Notice the three basic parts.

My Class

Topic Sentence

The students in my class come from many different parts of the world.

Supporting Sentences

Some students are from European countries, such as Germany and Italy, and others are from Middle Eastern countries, such as Saudi Arabia and Turkey. Several students were born in Latin American countries, including Peru and Brazil. Most students are from Asian countries, such as Korea, China, and Japan.

Concluding Sentence

My classmates are an interesting mix of people from many different countries, and we all get along very well.

A paragraph must be written in a proper form. Follow these rules.

- Indent the first word of each paragraph 1/2 inch.
- Leave margins (space on both sides of the paragraph).
- Begin each sentence with a capital letter.
- End each sentence with a period, question mark, or exclamation point.
- The sentences in a paragraph follow each other on the same line. (Do not start each sentence on a new line.)

PRACTICE **Read the model paragraphs and answer the questions.**

1.

> There are many reasons why people move. Some people move to find better jobs or to advance their careers. Others are attracted to places with better weather. Still others want to move to a place with less crime. Finally, people often want to move to a place with a lower cost of living. For these reasons, every year millions of people move to new places.

a. What is the topic sentence? _____

_____

b. How many supporting sentences are there in the paragraph? _____

c. What is the concluding sentence? _____

_____

2.

> More men are now doing jobs that traditionally belonged to women. For example, there are now twice as many male nurses as there were thirty years ago. The number of stay-at-home fathers in the United States has increased from 98,000 in 2003 to more than 200,000 today. Similarly, there are many more male secretaries, elementary school teachers, librarians, and bank tellers than ever before. It is clear that ideas about traditionally female occupations have changed.

a. What is the topic sentence? _____

_____

b. How many supporting sentences are there in the paragraph? _____

c. What is the concluding sentence? _____

_____

3.

> For thousands of years, garlic has had many uses. The Romans gave garlic to their slaves for strength and to their soldiers for courage. During the Middle Ages, some people used garlic to keep witches away. In the eighteenth century, garlic was used to cure diseases. Even today, some people believe that eating garlic can prevent colds. Garlic has a long history as a plant with many uses.

a. What is the topic sentence? _____

_____

b. How many supporting sentences are there in the paragraph? _____

c. What is the concluding sentence? _____

_____

4.

> Today, cell phones can do a lot more than just make and receive calls. Most cell phones come with cameras that take color pictures. Many also have video cameras to record live-action events. You can also use a cell phone to check your email, surf the Internet, or set reminders for important events with a special alarm clock. Many cell phones have calculators for solving math problems and fun games to play if you're bored. With all of these new features, it is hard to imagine what cell phones of the future will be able to do.

a. What is the topic sentence? _____

_____

b. How many supporting sentences are there in the paragraph? _____

c. What is the concluding sentence? _____

_____

5.

> The popular game of chess has a long and interesting history. No one knows for sure when chess was invented, but people were playing chess in China and India about 1,400 years ago. From Asia, chess spread to North Africa and then to Europe. The modern form of chess, which we play today, developed in the 1500s in Europe. Today, people around the world still play chess with each other or even on their computers. With its long history, chess will probably remain a popular game in the future.

a. What is the topic sentence? _____

_____

b. How many supporting sentences are there in the paragraph? _____

c. What is the concluding sentence? _____

_____

TOPIC SENTENCES

The *topic sentence* is the most important sentence of a paragraph. It states the main idea and introduces the reader to the topic. The topic sentence is more general than the other sentences in the paragraph. Remember that a topic sentence, like all English sentences, must have a subject and a verb.

A topic sentence should have two parts: the *topic* and the *controlling idea*. The topic states the subject of the paragraph. It is what the paragraph is about. The controlling idea limits the topic. It tells what you are going to say about the subject.

Read the following three topic sentences. Each one has the same topic—cell phones—but a different controlling idea.

┌ Topic ┐┌ Controlling Idea ┐

a. Cell phones make communication much easier.

┌ Topic ┐┌ Controlling Idea ┐

b. Cell phones are an annoying invention.

┌ Topic ┐┌ Controlling Idea ┐

c. Cell phones keep improving every year.

PRACTICE **(A)** **Draw a circle around the topic and underline the controlling idea in each sentence.**

1. Written exams make me nervous.

2. Colors have different meanings around the world.

3. Miles Davis is my favorite jazz musician.

4. There are several advantages to growing up in a small town.

5. The computer was the greatest invention of the twentieth century.

6. The Cannes Film Festival is the largest and most famous film festival in the world.

7. My proudest moment came the day I received the sportsmanship award.

(B) **Complete each topic sentence by adding a controlling idea.**

1. Good drivers _____

2. Public transportation _____

3. Television _____

4. My parents _____

5. My first day of school _____

6. My most embarrassing moment _____

Identifying Topic Sentences

PRACTICE Choose the best topic sentence for each paragraph. Write it on the line provided.

1. <u>*Skiing is my favorite sport.*</u> I usually go skiing every weekend in the winter even though it is expensive. I love the feeling of flying down a mountain. The views are beautiful from the top of a mountain and along the trails. Even the danger of falling and getting hurt can't keep me away from the slopes on a winter day.

    a. Skiing is expensive.

    b. Skiing is my favorite sport.

    c. Skiing is dangerous.

2. _____ North Americans send cards for many occasions. They send cards to family and friends on birthdays and holidays. They also send thank-you cards, get-well cards, graduation cards, and congratulation cards. It is very common to buy cards in stores and send them through the mail, but sending e-cards over the Internet is also popular.

    a. Sending cards is very popular in North America.

    b. Birthday cards are the most popular kind of card.

    c. It is important to send thank-you cards.

3. _____ I enjoy summer sports like water skiing and baseball. The weather is usually sunny and hot, so I can go to the beach almost every day. Gardening is my hobby, and I spend many summer days working in my garden. Unfortunately, the days pass too quickly in summer.

    a. I like to garden in the summer.

    b. Summer is my favorite season.

    c. Summer is too short.

4. _____ First of all, our coach is always late for practice so the team never has enough time to train. Also, he is very mean during the games and yells at the players rather than giving them advice on how to improve. Finally, our current coach doesn't even know how to play soccer well!

    a. My soccer team has a horrible coach.

    b. A good soccer coach should be able to play soccer well.

    c. Soccer is my favorite sport.

5. _____ For example, a person can have breakfast in New York and fly to Paris for dinner. A businesswoman in London can place an order with a factory in Hong Kong instantly by sending a text. People can use videocalls over the Internet to have a meeting without leaving their homes.

   a. Airplanes have changed our lives.

   b. Advances in technology have made the world seem smaller.

   c. The fax machine was an important invention.

6. _____ One thing you must consider is the quality of the university's educational program. You also need to think about the school's size and location. Finally, you must be sure to consider the university's tuition to make sure you can afford to go to school there.

   a. It is expensive to attend a university in the United States.

   b. You should consider getting a good education.

   c. There are several factors to consider when you choose a university to attend.

7. _____ One type of reality television show is the competition-based program. In these shows, contestants go through a series of challenges, and whoever wins the most challenges at the end of the season gets a big prize. Another type of popular reality show is the documentary-based type. In these shows, viewers watch people going about their daily lives and facing everyday challenges. Finally, there are instructional reality shows. For example, there are shows that can teach you how to cook a delicious meal in thirty minutes or redecorate your living room without spending too much money.

   a. There are many types of reality shows on television today.

   b. Reality shows are my favorite type of television programs.

   c. Anyone can learn to cook just by watching television.

Writing Topic Sentences

WRITER'S TIP: Topic Sentence

Here is a test you can use to make sure you have a good topic and supporting sentences. Turn your topic sentence into a question. The rest of the paragraph should answer this question. If the rest of your paragraph doesn't answer this question, then your topic sentence probably doesn't fit the content of the paragraph, or the other sentences don't support the topic sentence.

PRACTICE Write a topic sentence for each of the following paragraphs. Make sure your topic sentence includes a topic and a controlling idea. Then share your topic sentences with your classmates by writing them on the board. Discuss the differences.

1. _Miami is the perfect place to take a vacation._ It is always sunny and warm. The beaches are gorgeous, with soft white sand and beautiful water. There are many fine restaurants in the Miami area, and most of the hotels offer terrific nightly entertainment. It's no wonder that Miami is my first choice for a vacation destination.

2. _____ He has collected stamps and coins ever since he was a child. He is very proud of his valuable collections. Paul also enjoys painting and drawing. Recently he has become interested in gardening. Out of all of his hobbies, Paul's favorite one is reading. He usually reads at least one book every week. Paul keeps busy with all of his hobbies.

3. _____ I can't wait to come home from school and eat the delicious meals she has prepared. My mother is famous for her desserts, like peach pie and chocolate soufflé. She is always experimenting with new recipes and trying different ingredients. No one in the world can cook the way my mother does.

4. _____ First, and most importantly, the work is very interesting. I learn new things every day and I get to travel a lot. In addition, my boss is very nice. She is always willing to help me when I have a problem. I have also made many new friends at my job. Last but not least, the salary is fantastic. I plan on staying at this job for a long time.

5. _____ For one thing, feathers help birds by keeping them warm and dry. Colorful feathers also play an important part in attracting mates. The colors of a bird's feathers can also provide camouflage and protect it from predators. Finally, the main purpose of feathers is to help birds fly.

6. _____ By sending Twitter updates, I was able to let my family and friends know where I was on my adventure in Turkey. Even though I was thousands of miles away, I could update my family and friends with quick "tweets" on my status. I also enjoyed reading the comments that my friends and family posted on my tweets. I followed my friends' tweets and stayed informed on their lives, too. Twitter was a quick and easy way for me to describe my experiences and keep up to date on my friends as I traveled in Turkey.

SUPPORTING SENTENCES

The *supporting sentences* develop the main idea stated in the topic sentence. The supporting details are more specific than the main idea. Their purpose is to help readers understand more about your main idea. Supporting sentences can give examples, facts, explanations, or reasons. Supporting sentences often tell *who, what, when, where, why, how, how much,* or *how many*.

Identifying Supporting Sentences

PRACTICE **Read the following paragraphs and underline the supporting sentences.**

1.
Use of the Internet has grown very quickly. In 1983, there were 562 computers connected to the Internet, but by the turn of the century, there were 361 million computers in 247 countries online. Experts say that the Internet is now growing at a rate of approximately 50 to 60 percent a year. They predict that by 2018 there will be 3.6 billion connected computers. As time goes on, the Internet continues to become more and more popular.

2.

There are many reasons that I hate my apartment. First of all, the windows are small and the apartment is never sunny. I also have noisy neighbors who keep me up all night. The air conditioner doesn't work properly, so it's too hot in the summer. Finally, there are so many bugs in my apartment that I could start an insect collection. I really want to move!

3.

Vegetables and fruits are an important part of a healthy diet. First, fruits and vegetables are packed with the vitamins and minerals you need to keep your body functioning smoothly. In addition, they give you the carbohydrates you need for energy. Fruits and vegetables have lots of fiber to help your digestive system work properly. Finally, many scientists believe that the nutrients in fruits and vegetables can help fight diseases. If you eat a diet rich in fruits and vegetables, you'll be on the road to better health.

Writing Supporting Sentences

PRACTICE **Write three supporting sentences for each topic sentence. Compare your sentences with a partner's.**

1. There are several reasons why I am learning English.

   a. _____

   b. _____

   c. _____

2. My hometown is an interesting (or boring) place to visit.

   a. _____

   b. _____

   c. _____

3. I am usually an optimistic (or pessimistic) person.

   a. _____

   b. _____

   c. _____

4. My best friend is a serious (or fun-loving) person.

   a. _____

   b. _____

   c. _____

CONCLUDING SENTENCES

Some paragraphs end with a *concluding sentence*. This sentence often restates the main idea of the paragraph using different words. It summarizes the main points of the paragraph or makes a final comment on the topic. Although concluding sentences are common, they are not always necessary. For example, some short paragraphs or paragraphs that are part of longer pieces of writing often do not have concluding sentences.

Choosing Concluding Sentences

PRACTICE **Choose the best concluding sentence for each paragraph. Write it on the line.**

1.   Kimchi is the most popular food in Korea. In fact, Koreans serve kimchi as a side dish at almost every meal. Kimchi is made of pickled vegetables and spices, and it's very hot and spicy. Koreans enjoy more than 100 different kinds of kimchi! This delicious food can be eaten alone or mixed with rice or noodles. Luckily, since I eat a lot of it, kimchi is very nutritious. It has vitamins, lactic acid, and minerals. _____

   a. If you visit Korea, I hope you will try kimchi.

   b. I love all kinds of spicy food.

   c. Pho is the most popular food in Vietnam.

2.   My sister Ellen is one of the worst drivers I know. First of all, she is always talking on her cell phone while she drives. To make matters worse, she doesn't pay attention to road signs or speed limits. Sometimes, she puts on lipstick while she's at a red light and doesn't notice when the light turns green. Finally, she often forgets to use her turn signal when she's making a turn.

   _____

   a. I won't be surprised if Ellen gets into an accident soon.

   b. Ellen has never gotten a speeding ticket.

   c. Ellen's new car is a hybrid; it uses less gas than a regular car.

3.   Breakfast is the most important meal of the day. After sleeping all night, breakfast gives your body the boost of energy it needs to start the day. Eating a healthy breakfast helps you think more clearly and even improves your memory. Studies show that children who eat a nutritious breakfast are more alert and do better in school. Similarly, adults who eat breakfast perform better at work.

   _____

   a. Some people skip breakfast and eat a big dinner.

   b. Children who study hard usually do better in school.

   c. My mother was right all along when she said, "Remember to eat a good breakfast."

Writing Concluding Sentences

PRACTICE **Write a concluding sentence for each paragraph. Then share your concluding sentences with your classmates by writing them on the board. Discuss the differences.**

1. There are many reasons why I like wearing a uniform to school. First of all, it saves time. I don't have to spend time picking out my clothes every morning. Wearing a uniform also saves money. It's cheaper to purchase a few uniforms than to go out and buy lots of school clothes. In addition, I don't have the pressure of keeping up with the latest styles. Most importantly, wearing a school uniform gives me a sense that I belong. I really think it adds to the feeling of school spirit and community. _____

2. There are many reasons why I am against wearing my school uniform. For one thing, I don't like the style of the uniform. The navy blazer and plaid skirt are too conservative for me. Secondly, the uniform isn't comfortable. I prefer to wear baggy pants and a sweater instead of a skirt and jacket. Finally, I want the freedom to express my individuality through my style of dressing.

    _____

3. Credit cards have a lot of advantages. First of all, credit cards are convenient because you don't have to carry a lot of cash around. You can buy the products and services you need even if you do not have cash in your pocket. In addition, credit cards are very helpful in emergencies. Finally, you can become a better money manager as you learn to use credit cards responsibly.

    _____

4. I don't use credit cards anymore for several reasons. First of all, credit cards enable me to spend more money than I have. When I get the bill, I never have enough money in the bank to pay the whole amount. That leads to the second problem—the high interest rate credit card companies charge. Every month I end up paying a lot of money in interest on the amount I still owe on my account. Finally, credit cards are not always the safest way to pay for things. If someone gets your credit card number or steals your card, you may be a victim of credit card fraud.

    _____

ORGANIZING INFORMATION AND TOPIC SENTENCES

PRACTICE **A** Read and discuss the following sentences about Springfield Academy, a boarding school for high school students. Four of the sentences are about the quality of education. Label these *Q*. Four are about the rules of the school. Label these *R*. Four sentences relate to the athletic department. Label these *A*.

__Q__ 1. Springfield Academy is famous for the high quality of its education.

_____ 2. The athletic director and all the team coaches are excellent.

_____ 3. Students are not allowed to leave campus without permission.

_____ 4. Every year several Springfield graduates receive athletic scholarships to college.

_____ 5. Students are required to wear uniforms.

_____ 6. The library and laboratories have the newest computers and equipment.

_____ 7. Most of its graduates attend very good universities.

_____ 8. It has a new gymnasium, an Olympic-size pool, clay tennis courts, and great playing fields.

_____ 9. Many of the students at Springfield Academy feel that the rules are too strict.

_____ 10. Students who do not maintain a B average are put on probation.

_____ 11. The teachers and academic counselors are excellent.

_____ 12. Springfield Academy is known for its wonderful athletic department.

B Divide the sentences from Exercise A into three groups. Remember to put similar ideas together. One sentence in each group is general enough to be a topic sentence. Put a check (✔) next to that sentence.

Quality of Education

✔ Springfield Academy is famous for the high quality of its education.

The library and laboratories have the newest computers and equipment.

_____

_____

Rules of the School

_____

_____

_____

_____

_____

_____

_____

_____

C Write the sentences from the first group, Quality of Education. Begin with the topic sentence. Then write the supporting sentences. Add your own concluding sentence.

_____

_____

_____

_____

_____

_____

D Write the sentences from the second group, Rules of the School. Begin with the topic sentence. Then write the supporting sentences. Add your own concluding sentence.

_____

_____

_____

_____

_____

_____

E Write the sentences from the third group, Athletic Department. Begin with the topic sentence. Then write the supporting sentences. Add your own concluding sentence.

_____

_____

_____

_____

_____

_____

_____

Identifying Topic and Supporting Sentences

PRACTICE **A** **Read the following sentences about San Francisco. Discuss them with your partner. Two of the sentences are topic sentences, and the rest are supporting sentences. Write *TS* in front of each topic sentence and *SS* in front of each supporting sentence.**

_SS_ 1. San Francisco is usually warm and pleasant during the day.

_____ 2. Some of the country's most famous restaurants and hotels are in San Francisco.

_____ 3. There are many things to see and do in San Francisco.

_____ 4. There are many interesting tourist attractions, such as Fisherman's Wharf and the Golden Gate Bridge.

_____ 5. It is never too hot or too cold.

_____ 6. The weather in San Francisco is very pleasant.

_____ 7. The nightlife is exciting.

_____ 8. San Francisco has art galleries, a ballet company, an opera house, and an orchestra.

_____ 9. It is cool and breezy at night.

_____ 10. The winters are mild and it rarely snows.

B **Write the two topic sentences on the lines provided. Then list the supporting sentences under the topic sentences.**

Topic Sentence 1

_____

Supporting Sentences

_San Francisco is usually warm and pleasant during the day._____

_____

_____

_____

Topic Sentence 2

_____

Supporting Sentences

_____

_____

_____

_____

C Write the sentences with the first topic sentence in paragraph form. Add your own concluding sentence.

_____

_____

_____

_____

_____

_____

_____

D Now write the sentences with the second topic sentence in paragraph form. Add your own concluding sentence.

_____

_____

_____

_____

_____

_____

_____

PARAGRAPH UNITY

Read this paragraph again. Cross out the irrelevant sentence.

My Class

The students in my class come from many different parts of the world. Some students are from European countries, such as Germany and Italy, and others are from Middle Eastern countries, such as Saudi Arabia and Turkey. Several students were born in Latin American countries, including Peru and Brazil. The food in Mexico is delicious. Most students are from Asian countries, such as Korea, China, and Japan. My classmates are an interesting mix of people from many different countries, and we all get along very well.

The main idea of the paragraph above is that the students in the class come from many different parts of the world. A sentence about Mexican food is interesting, but it does not support the main idea. It is irrelevant. Which sentence discusses Mexican food? Did you cross out that sentence?

PRACTICE **Read the following sentences. Put a check (✔) next to each sentence that could be added to the paragraph in A because it supports the main idea.**

_____ 1. Several of the students are from African countries.

_____ 2. Half of the students are women.

_____ 3. A few of the students were born in Turkey.

_____ 4. Two students are from Indonesia.

_____ 5. Most of the students are between eighteen and twenty-five years old.

Identifying Irrelevant Sentences

One sentence in each paragraph does not relate to the topic. Find that sentence and cross it out.

1.

Wonderful House Pets

Cats make wonderful house pets. They are very loving and friendly. Cats are also clean. They don't eat much, so they are not expensive to feed. Unfortunately, some people are allergic to their hair. Cats look beautiful, and they're fun to have in your home.

2.

How to Conserve Natural Resources

There are several ways people can conserve natural resources. One way is to turn off lights and appliances when they are not in use. Another way is to drive cars less often so they use less gas. My favorite kind of car is a convertible. People can also insulate their houses better. Finally, by reusing things like bottles and plastic bags, people can reduce the amount of waste they create. By practicing these simple guidelines, we can save our natural resources.

3.

Capital Cities

The capital city of a country is usually a very important city. The government offices are located in the capital city, and political leaders usually live there or nearby. There are many different types of governments in the world. The capital may also be the center of culture. There are often museums, libraries, and universities in the capital. Finally, the capital city can serve as a center of trade, industry, and commerce, so it is often the financial center of the country.

4.

Using Robots in Japanese Auto Factories

The Japanese automobile industry uses robots in many stages of its production process. In fact, one large Japanese auto factory uses robots in all of its production stages. Some Japanese universities are developing medical robots to detect certain kinds of cancer. Another automobile factory in Japan uses some robots to paint cars as they come off the assembly line, and other robots to perform tasks such as glass attachment, interior panel installation, seat mounting, and door fitting. Furthermore, most Japanese factories use robots to weld the parts of the finished car together.

5.

Wasteful Packaging

The packaging of many products is very wasteful. Often the packaging is twice as big as the product. Packaging is used to protect things that are breakable. Many food items, for example, have several layers of extra packaging, but most of these layers are unnecessary. Most of these extra layers could and should be eliminated, especially since packaging accounts for most of the litter found on streets, in streams, and in parks. I hope companies will start to pay more attention to the way their products are packaged.

GRAMMAR FOR WRITING: Compound Sentences

When you write in English you can combine two simple sentences using *coordinating conjunctions* such as *and*, *but*, *so*, and *or* to make *compound sentences*. This will make your writing more interesting because you will have a variety of types of sentences. The coordinating conjunctions will also help the reader understand the connection between ideas.

Study the chart.

COORDINATING CONJUNCTION	PURPOSE	EXAMPLE
and	joins two similar ideas together	Jane and Catherine went to a movie, **and** they really enjoyed it.
but	joins two contrasting ideas	I wanted to go to the party, **but** I was too sick.
so	connects a reason and a result	Jenny misses her parents, **so** she keeps a picture of them on her desk.
or	joins two alternative ideas	You can call me, **or** you can send me an email.

Note: Most compound sentences have a comma (,) before the coordinating conjunction.

 PRACTICE **A** Look at the paragraph "My Class" on page 25 and underline the compound sentences.

B Look at the paragraphs on pages 26 and 27. Underline the compound sentences. Circle the coordinating conjunctions.

C Work in a small group. Compare the compound sentences you have identified. Discuss what the coordinating conjunctions do. For example, do they join similar ideas? Connect a reason and a result?

D Work with a partner. Combine each set of sentences into a compound sentence with a coordinating conjunction.

1. Australia is the smallest continent. It has many types of landscapes.

   Australia is the smallest continent, but it has many types of landscapes.

2. Our computers are old and outdated. We are raising money to buy new ones.

   _____

   _____

3. Children enter the world lacking the skills to take care of themselves. Parents must nurture and protect children when they are young.

   _____

   _____

4. The family is the basic social unit in every culture. Its structure varies widely among different cultures.

   _____

   _____

5. Women around the world have won important rights during the last hundred years. Gender inequality still exists in many places.

   _____

   _____

6. Scientists from all over the world go to Antarctica to study the weather and climate. They go to research the geology and wildlife.

   _____

   _____

7. In the early days of photography, cameras were big and bulky. Pictures were made on individual glass plates.

   _____

   _____

8. I have been trying to lose weight for several months. I can't stop eating fattening things like cookies and sodas.

   _____

   _____

WRITING PARAGRAPHS

Paragraph Practice 1

A **Work with your classmates. Read the following topic sentence.**

It is difficult to learn a new language.

What ideas can you and your classmates think of to support this topic sentence? As you think of ideas, your teacher will write them in list form on the board. Remember, these are just ideas, so they don't have to be complete sentences or in correct order. Copy the list here.

_____

_____

_____

_____

_____

B **Discuss the list with your classmates. Cross out details that don't belong.**

C **With your classmates and teacher, choose the best ideas from your list. Write them in sentence form on the board. Copy the sentences onto the following lines.**

_____

_____

_____

_____

_____

D **With your classmates and teacher, organize the sentences and put them in correct paragraph form. Your teacher will write the paragraph on the board. Try to include some compound sentences in your paragraph. Copy the finished paragraph here.**

_____

_____

_____

_____

_____

_____

_____

Paragraph Practice 2

(A) **Choose one of the following topic sentences to write about.**

- Good teachers have several important qualities.
- There are several ways to save money when you take a vacation.
- _____ is a great place to visit.

(B) **Make a list of supporting ideas. You do not have to write the list in complete sentences.**

_____

_____

_____

_____

_____

(C) **Cross out any ideas that do not support the topic sentence. Write the items on your list in complete sentences.**

_____

_____

_____

_____

_____

(D) **Write a paragraph based on your list. Remember to begin with the topic sentence. Include at least one compound sentence. Add a concluding sentence at the end of your paragraph.**

_____

_____

_____

_____

_____

_____

_____

(E) **Form small groups and share your paragraph with the other members of your group.**

YOU BE THE EDITOR

Read the paragraph. It contains eleven mistakes. Correct the mistakes. Copy the corrected paragraph on a separate piece of paper.

Erik's Favorite Sports

Erik enjoy many types of sports. He is liking team sports such as basketball, soccer, and baseball. In fact, he is the Captain of the basketball team at our school. erik also plays individual sports like squash, tennis, and golf very good. Last year, he win two golf tournaments and most of the tennis matches he played. His favorites sports involve dangerous as well as excitement. He is no afraid to go extreme skiing or skydiving. He is an excellent athlete, it was not a surprise when Erik won the sports award at graduation.

ON YOUR OWN

Write a paragraph about one of the following topics.

- your proudest or most embarrassing moment
- your best or worst job
- your best friend
- your favorite kind of music, movies, literature, or art

Follow these steps.

1. Write a topic sentence.

2. Make a list of supporting details.

3. Think about the ideas on your list. Cross out any ideas that do not support your topic sentence.

4. Write your list in complete sentences.

5. Use the topic and supporting sentences to write a paragraph.

6. Write a concluding sentence.

CHAPTER 3

Organizing Information by Time Order

LEARNING OUTCOME **Paragraph Writing:** Write a paragraph organized by time order

In Chapter 1, you learned that organization is the key to good writing. There are several ways to organize sentences in a paragraph. Three common ways include:

- time order
- order of importance
- spatial order

In this chapter you will practice organizing ideas and sentences by time order. When you tell a story, you organize the events in the story as they occur in time. You tell what happens first at the beginning of the story. Then you tell what happens second, third, and so on. In writing, you often do the same thing.

"Thank you for calling. Please leave a message.
In case I forget to check my messages, please
email an audio file, then send me a Facebook
message to remind me to check my email, then
text me to make sure I'm on Facebook and
call me back to make sure I got your text."

TIME ORDER

Read the model paragraph and answer the questions.

A Terrible Day

I had a terrible day yesterday. First, I woke up an hour late because my alarm clock didn't go off. From then on, everything went wrong. I burned my hand when I was making breakfast. After I ate breakfast, I got dressed so quickly that I forgot to wear socks. Next, I ran out of the house trying to get the 9:30 bus, but, of course, I missed it. I wanted to take a taxi, but I didn't have enough money. Finally, I walked the 3 miles to my office only to discover that it was Sunday! I hope I never have a day as bad as the one I had yesterday.

1. What is the topic sentence?

   _____

2. How many supporting sentences are there? They are organized by time order. How do you know?

   _____

3. What is the concluding sentence?

   _____

WRITER'S TIP: Signal Words

A well-organized paragraph often includes signal words (also called *transitions*) to connect ideas in a paragraph. Signal words help guide the reader from one idea to the next. They are like traffic signals that help you when you are driving. There are many types of signal words. When you write a paragraph using time order, you should use some *time order signal words* to explain the order of events.

SIGNAL WORDS THAT SHOW TIME ORDER

after	before	first	later	second
after that	finally	last	next	then

There are other ways of showing time order, too. You can include dates, months, years, times, or other time phrases to show the order of events.

OTHER SIGNALS OF TIME ORDER

on January 1, 2012	in March	for three months	at noon
several years later	on Wednesday	at the end of May	at the beginning of July

A Underline the signal words in the paragraph "A Terrible Day" on page 33.

B Complete the paragraph with signal words.

My Busy Mornings

Mornings are my busiest time of day. _____ my alarm goes off at 6 A.M. and I jump out of bed. _____ I rush to the kitchen to make breakfast for my husband and children. _____ I wake everyone else up and get dressed for work. At 7:00 we eat a quick breakfast. I eat very quickly because right _____ breakfast, I have to pack lunches for my kids and make sure they are ready for school. My husband leaves for work at 7:30. Luckily, he drops the kids off at school so I have a few minutes to get myself together _____ I go to work. _____, I leave the house at 7:45 and rush to catch the 8 o'clock train to my office. By the time I sit down at my desk, I'm already exhausted.

RECOGNIZING TIME ORDER

A Look at the pictures. They tell a story, but they are not in the right order. Discuss the pictures with a partner and number them 1 to 4 so they tell the story in the right order. The student's name is Pedro.

a. _____ b. _____ c. _____ d. _____

B Write a sentence about each picture in Exercise A.

1. _____

2. _____

3. _____

4. _____

C **Read the topic sentence. Then read the sentences that follow it. Together they tell a story. The sentences are not in the correct order. Number them so they follow a logical time order. Then use all of the sentences to write a paragraph.**

1. José saved his money and spent two months traveling around the world.

   _____ He spent a week in New York and then flew to London and enjoyed several weeks in Europe.

   _____ Next, José took a train from London to Istanbul and visited many places in Asia.

   _1_ First, he flew from his home in Mexico City to New York City.

   _____ After he traveled through Asia, he went to South America and finally back home to Mexico.

Jose's Trip around the World

_____

_____

_____

_____

_____

2. Tim had a hard time keeping his New Year's resolutions.

   _____ Then, as the months went on, he broke even more resolutions.

   _____ On January 1, he wrote a list of New Year's resolutions.

   _____ At the end of January, Tim had broken half of the resolutions.

   _____ Finally, when the year ended, he realized that he had not kept a single resolution.

Broken New Year's Resolutions

_____

_____

_____

_____

3. Mark decided that he wanted to plant a vegetable garden.

   _____ Finally, at the end of the summer, he picked the vegetables from the garden.

   _____ First, he went to a garden store and bought seeds.

   _____ Then he went home, prepared the soil, and planted the seeds.

   _____ Later, Mark watered and weeded the garden.

_____

_____

_____

_____

GRAMMAR FOR WRITING: Prepositions of Time

Prepositions of time, such as *at*, *on*, and *in* are often used to show when something happened.

Study the chart.

RULES FOR PREPOSITIONS OF TIME	EXAMPLES
Use *at* with specific times.	**at** 5:00 / **at** 7:30 / **at** noon / **at** midnight
Use *from* and *to* with a span of time.	**from** 6:00 **to** 9:00 / **from** 1941 **to** 1945
Use *in* with other parts of the day.	**in** the afternoon / **in** the morning / **in** the evening (exception: **at** night / **at** midnight / **at** noon)
Use *in* with months.	**in** August / **in** June
Use *in* with years.	**in** 2009 / **in** 2010
Use *in* with seasons.	**in** the spring / **in** the summer / **in** the winter
Use *on* with days of the week.	**on** Sunday / **on** Tuesday / **on** Friday
Use *on* with specific dates.	**on** June 30 / **on** April 21, 2010 / **on** New Year's Eve

PRACTICE **A** **Circle the prepositions of time in the paragraph "My Busy Mornings" on page 34.**

B **Complete the sentences with the correct prepositions.**

1. I lived in Detroit _____ 1999 _____ 2012.

2. Lynn was born _____ 1984.

3. She was born _____ October 31, _____ 4:00

    _____ the afternoon.

4. I'll meet you for lunch _____ Tuesday _____ noon.

5. Ruth goes to New York every weekend. _____ Saturday she takes the train

    _____ 9:00 _____ the morning and arrives in New York

    at 10:45.

6. We usually go on vacation _____ the summer.

7. I went to a great party _____ New Year's Eve.

8. My children start school _____ September.

9. The cafeteria opens for lunch _____ noon.

C You saw this announcement for a Jon McLaughlin concert in the newspaper. Write an email to a friend. Tell your friend about the concert and invite him or her to go with you. Be sure to use correct prepositions of time.

World Café Live
Presents Jon McLaughlin
Come celebrate with us on New Year's Eve!
Friday, Dec. 31 at 10:00 P.M.
3025 Walnut St. • 215-555-1400 • $19–$24

To:
From:
Subject: Jon McLaughlin concert

Send   Reply   Reply all   Forward

WRITING PARAGRAPHS USING TIME ORDER

WRITER'S TIP: Writing Titles for Paragraphs

Many single paragraphs have a *title*. The purpose of the title is to give the reader an idea what the paragraph is about. A title of a paragraph tells the main idea in a few words. If a paragraph is part of a longer piece of writing, it does not need a title. Here are some things to remember when you write titles:

- Titles are not complete sentences.

- Always capitalize the first and last words of a title.

- Capitalize all other important words in the title including nouns, verbs, and adjectives. Do not capitalize articles (*a, an, the*) or prepositions (for example *to, from, at, with*)

- Do not use a period at the end of a title. Do not use quotation marks (" ") around the title. But you may use a question mark (?) or an exclamation point (!).

- Center the title over the paragraph.

PRACTICE **Correct the titles.**

1. my Busy morning _____

2. OUR NEW CLASSMATE. _____

3. "How to make a great omelet" _____

4. Spending quality Time With Friends and family _____

5. Fun On The Ski Slopes. _____

Paragraph Practice 1

Dr. Alden is the director of an English language school. Study his schedule for Tuesday, February 9. On a separate piece of paper, write a paragraph about his day. Remember to begin with a topic sentence. Use signal words to guide the reader. Include a title.

My Calendar	February 9
8:30–9:00	greet new students
9:00–10:30	give test to new students
10:30–11:30	order textbooks
11:30–12:00	check email
12:00–1:00	have lunch meeting with staff
1:00–3:00	observe classes
3:00–5:00	attend curriculum meeting
5:00–7:00	lead city tour with new students

Paragraph Practice 2

Vicki is having a birthday dinner for her friend. She made a list of things she has to do before the party. She put the things on her list in time order. Use her list to write a paragraph about the things she has to do. Remember to begin with a topic sentence. Use signal words to guide the reader. Include a title.

TO DO...   +

buy food for dinner at supermarket

pick up birthday cake at bakery

clean house

make dinner

wrap present

set table

_____

Paragraph Practice 3

**Vicki was busy the day after the big birthday party. Look
at her To-Do list and write a paragraph about her day.**

TO DO...   +

vacuum living room

empty the dishwasher

go to the gym

meet Mom for lunch

do laundry

study for Spanish test

_____

_____

_____

_____

_____

_____

_____

_____

_____

_____

_____

_____

_____

Paragraph Practice 4

Elizabeth Blackwell was the first female medical doctor in the United States. The following time line gives you information about her life. Use the timeline to write a paragraph about her life. Remember to begin with a topic sentence. Use signal words to guide the reader. Add a title.

February 3, 1821:	born in Bristol, England
1832:	emigrated to New York City
1849:	graduated from Geneva Medical School in Geneva, New York
1853:	opened the New York Infirmary because, as a woman, she could not get a job in a hospital
1868:	opened the Women's Medical College of the New York Infirmary
1875:	assisted in founding the London School of Medicine for Women
1910:	died in Hastings, England

_____

_____

_____

_____

_____

_____

_____

_____

_____

_____

_____

_____

Paragraph Practice 5

Yao Ming is a famous Chinese basketball player in America and the tallest person playing for the National Basketball Association. The following timeline gives you information about his life. Use the timeline to write a paragraph about his life. Remember to write a topic sentence and include signal words to guide the reader. Add a title.

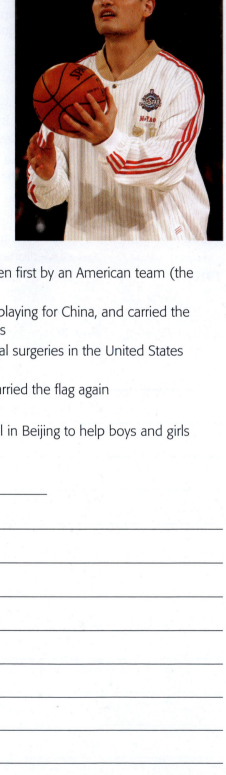

September 12, 1980:	born in Shanghai, China, to very tall parents who played basketball
1989:	entered a junior sports school in China and started to play basketball for the first time
1997:	joined the senior Shark Basketball Team in China and led them to their first championship
2002:	tried out for the NBA and became the first international player to be chosen first by an American team (the Houston Rockets)
2004:	participated in the Summer Olympics, playing for China, and carried the Chinese flag in the opening ceremonies
2005–2008:	broke his foot and knee and had several surgeries in the United States and China
Summer 2008:	played in the Olympics in China and carried the flag again
2011:	retired from the NBA due to foot injury
2014:	opened the NBA YAO basketball school in Beijing to help boys and girls learn good skills and teamwork

_____

_____

_____

_____

_____

_____

_____

_____

_____

_____

GRAMMAR FOR WRITING: Complex Sentences with *Before* and *After*

You have learned that a compound sentence is formed by joining two simple sentences with a coordinating conjunction. Another kind of sentence is called a **complex sentence**. A complex sentence is formed by joining an independent clause with a dependent clause.

An *independent clause* is a like a simple sentence. It has a subject and verb, and it expresses a complete thought.

A *dependent clause* also has a subject and verb, but it does not express a complete thought. A dependent clause always begins with a **subordinating conjunction**. There are many words in the English language that function as subordinating conjunctions. In this chapter, you will practice using two of them: *before* and *after*.

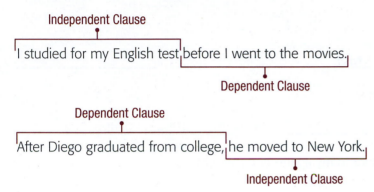

Independent Clause

I studied for my English test before I went to the movies.

Dependent Clause

Dependent Clause

After Diego graduated from college, he moved to New York.

Independent Clause

The dependent clause can come at the beginning or end of the sentence. When the dependent clause comes at the beginning of the sentence, use a comma to separate it from the independent clause.

Writers use *before* or *after* to introduce a dependent clause that tells when something happens in relation to the independent clause.

Study the chart.

EXPLANATION	EXAMPLES
After describes the first action of two or more actions.	I ate lunch at 12:30. I took a nap at 1:00. **After** I ate lunch, I took a nap. (This means: First, I ate lunch. Then, I took a nap.)
Before describes the second action of two or more actions.	I took a nap at 1:00. I went to the library at 2:00. **Before** I went to the library, I took a nap. (This means: First I took a nap. Then I went to the library.)

Look at the schedule. Write complex sentences with *before* or *after*, based on the schedule. Put the dependent time clause first.

7:00 A.M.	got up	10:00 A.M.	checked in	12:15 P.M.	took a nap
7:15 A.M.	ate breakfast	10:15 A.M.	waited at my gate	2:00 P.M.	The plane landed.
7:45 A.M.	got dressed	11:30 A.M.	The plane took off.	2:10 P.M.	called my friend to pick me up
9:00 A.M.	drove to airport	11:45 A.M.	read a magazine	2:20 P.M.	got off the plane

1. I ate breakfast. I got dressed. (before)

   Before I got dressed, I ate breakfast.

2. I drove to the airport. I got dressed. (after)

   _____

3. I turned off all the lights. I locked the door to my apartment. (before)

   _____

4. I drove to the airport. I checked in. (after)

   _____

5. I checked in. I waited at my gate. (after)

   _____

6. The plane took off. I waited and read a magazine. (before)

   _____

7. The plane landed. I called my friend to pick me up. (after)

   _____

8. I called my friend to pick me up. I got off the plane. (before)

   _____

PUTTING IT ALL TOGETHER

1. **Choose a memorable day in your life. Make a list of the important events of the day. Organize your list according to time order.**

   _____   _____

   _____   _____

   _____   _____

   _____   _____

2. **Write a topic sentence for your paragraph. You may fill in the blanks in the following sample or write your own.**

   _____ was one of the _____ days of my life.

3. **Use your list to write a paragraph about the day you chose. Don't forget to begin with a topic sentence and use signal words to guide the reader. Include at least one complex sentence with a dependent time clause. Add a title.**

   _____

   _____

   _____

   _____

   _____

   _____

   _____

   _____

   _____

   _____

   _____

   _____

YOU BE THE EDITOR

Read the paragraph. It contains eleven mistakes. Correct the mistakes. Copy the corrected paragraph on a separate piece of paper.

Mathematics throughout history

Throughout history, people have done mathematical computations and kept accounts. in early times, people used groups of sticks or stones to help make calculations. Then the abacus was developed in china. This simple method represents the beginnings of data processing? As computational needs became more complicated, people developed more advanced technologies. On 1642, Blaise pascal developed the first simple adding machine in france. Later, in England in 1830, charles Babbage designed the first machine that did calculations and printed out results. Finally, In the middle of the twentieth century, researchers at the University of pennsylvania built the first electronic computer. Today, of course, we have the computer to perform all kinds of advanced mathematical computations.

ON YOUR OWN

Choose a famous person who interests you. Find information about his or her life. Make a timeline based on the information and write a time order paragraph.

....
LEARNING OUTCOME **Paragraph Writing:** Write a paragraph listing the supporting ideas in order of importance
....

Another common way to organize information is by order of importance. When you use this pattern, you list your ideas from most important to least important or from least important to most important.

© Randy Glasbergen
www.glasbergen.com

"I made a list of 100 things I need to do this week and numbered them in order of imporance. Unfortunately, 99 are ranked #1."

ORDER OF IMPORTANCE

Read the model paragraph and answer the questions.

A Great Experience

Volunteering for an organization called Habitat for Humanity was one of the best experiences of my life. First of all, spending the summer helping to build a house taught me a lot of new skills. These skills are helpful because I plan to get a job in construction. Secondly, I met many new people working on the project. Some of them became good friends. Most importantly, I found personal satisfaction helping others. Volunteering really helped me as much as it helped the people who are moving into the house I helped build. I'll never forget my experience at Habitat for Humanity.

1. What is the topic sentence?

   _____

2. What three reasons does the author give to support the main idea?

   a. _____

   b. _____

   c. _____

3. Where does the author put the most important reason?

   _____

Topic Sentences for Order of Importance Paragraphs

Like all other paragraphs, an order of importance paragraph needs a good *topic sentence*. The topic sentence should come first, and it should be clear and to the point. The topic sentence often states that you are going to list different reasons (advantages, methods, etc.) to support your main idea.

Look at these example topic sentences for a paragraph organized around order of importance. Notice the phrases that are used to introduce the topic sentence.

Examples:

There are three reasons that I decided to attend Thompson University.

There are several things to consider when you purchase a new computer.

There are a number of ways to improve your vocabulary.

I like to study in the library *for several reasons*.

Walking to work *has several benefits*.

> **WRITER'S TIP:** Gerunds in Topic Sentences
>
> Notice the word *walking* in the topic sentence *Walking to work has several benefits*. *Walking* is a **gerund**. A gerund is a verb form that can be used as a noun. Gerunds are formed by adding *-ing* to the base form of a verb. Gerunds can be used as the subject of a sentence. In fact, gerunds are often the subject of topic sentences.

PRACTICE Write a topic sentence for an order of importance paragraph about each of the topics. Then compare your topic sentences in a small group.

1. exercising at a gym

   _____

2. save money

   _____

3. a college education

_____

4. cold weather

_____

5. playing team sports

_____

6. working part-time during college

_____

7. classical music

_____

8. live in a big city

_____

9. working for a small company

_____

10. a perfect roommate

_____

SIGNALING SUPPORTING POINTS

WRITER'S TIP: Adding New Ideas

Remember that *signal words* are words or phrases used to connect one idea to the next. Signal words help the reader understand your paragraph more easily. When you write paragraphs organized by order of importance, you should include signal words when you add a new supporting idea.

Study the list of signal words.

ORDER OF IMPORTANCE SIGNAL WORDS		
first	secondly	another (way, reason, example)
first of all	thirdly	also
for one thing	the most important (way, reason, example)	finally
	most importantly	in addition
		one (way, reason, example)
		the next (way, reason, example)

PRACTICE **A** Underline the signal words in the paragraph "A Great Experience" on page 47.

B Complete the following paragraph with signal words.

> ### Benefits of Riding a Bicycle
>
> There are three reasons that riding a bicycle can be a great alternative to driving a car. _____, you get a lot more exercise by riding a bicycle than by sitting behind the wheel of a car. _____, bicycles are less expensive than cars since they don't use gas and they cost less to repair. _____, bicycles are better for the environment because they don't cause pollution.

ORDERING SUPPORTING POINTS

PRACTICE **A** In a small group, discuss the topics below. Talk about the supporting ideas for each topic. Decide which is the most important. Put a *1* in front of it. Decide the next most important point and put a *2* in front of it, and so on. Use the list to complete each paragraph. Make sure you write the supporting ideas as complete sentences. You may begin with the most important idea or save it for last. Include signal words.

1. **Topic:** qualities of a good teacher

   Supporting Points:

   _____ has knowledge of subject

   _____ cares about students

   _____ can explain information clearly

Qualities of a Good Teacher

A good teacher has several important qualities. First of all, a good teacher _____

_____

_____

_____

_____

_____

_____

2. **Topic:** things to consider when you choose a university

Supporting Points:

_____ cost of attending the school

_____ location of the school

_____ quality of education

_____ number of students

Choosing a University

There are four important things to consider when you choose a university. _____

_____

_____

_____

_____

_____

_____

3. **Topic:** how to do well in school

Supporting Points:

_____ attend all classes

_____ take good notes

_____ complete all assignments

_____ study for exams in advance (don't cram)

How to Succeed in School

There are several things you should do so that you will succeed in school. _____

_____

_____

_____

_____

_____

_____

B For the next three paragraphs, discuss the topics and supporting points with your group. Write your own topic sentences. Number the supporting points in order of importance. Make sure you write the supporting ideas as complete sentences and use signal words when you write your paragraph. Include a title.

1. **Topic:** difficult things about living in a foreign country

   Supporting Points:

   _____ learning a new language

   _____ adjusting to unfamiliar customs

   _____ using different money

   _____ feeling homesick

   _____

   _____

   _____

   _____

   _____

   _____

   _____

   _____

2. **Topic:** benefits of a higher education

   Supporting Points:

   _____ have more employment opportunities

   _____ earn higher salary

   _____ gain prestige

   _____ learn valuable information

   _____

   _____

   _____

   _____

   _____

   _____

   _____

3. **Topic:** how to make a good impression at a job interview

Supporting Points:

_____ be on time

_____ come prepared

_____ ask questions

_____ be polite

_____ dress appropriately

_____

_____

_____

_____

_____

_____

_____

C For the next three paragraphs, discuss the topic with your group and write your own supporting ideas. Number the ideas according to order of importance. Then write a paragraph based on your list. Remember to begin with a topic sentence and to include signal words. Add a title.

1. **Topic:** things to consider when renting an apartment or buying a house

Supporting Points:

_____ _____

_____ _____

_____ _____

_____ _____

_____

_____

_____

_____

_____

_____

2. **Topic:** advantages of learning a foreign language

   Supporting Points:

   ____ _____

   ____ _____

   ____ _____

   ____ _____

   _____

   _____

   _____

   _____

   _____

   _____

3. **Topic:** qualities of a good neighbor

   Supporting Points:

   ____ _____

   ____ _____

   ____ _____

   ____ _____

   _____

   _____

   _____

   _____

   _____

   _____

GRAMMAR FOR WRITING: Correcting Comma Splices

In Chapter 2, you learned how to join two simple sentences with a coordinating conjunction and a comma to make one compound sentence. However, a common mistake is to join two simple sentences with only a comma and no coordinating conjunction. This is called a *comma splice*. It is easy to make this mistake when the two simple sentences are related to each other.

There are two easy ways to correct comma splice mistakes.

SOLUTIONS	EXAMPLES
You can add a coordinating conjunction such as *and*, *but*, *so*, and *or* and keep the comma. When you do this you will have one compound sentence.	• INCORRECT (comma splice): I went home early, I practiced the piano. • CORRECT: I went home early, and I practiced the piano. • INCORRECT (comma splice): I didn't clean my room, my mother was angry. • CORRECT: I didn't clean my room, so my mother was angry.
You can also correct the comma splice by changing the comma to a period. This way creates two simple sentences. Remember to begin each sentence with a capital letter.	• INCORRECT (comma splice): Lois wants to watch a movie, her roommate wants to watch the soccer match. • CORRECT: Lois wants to watch a movie. Her roommate wants to watch the soccer match.

PRACTICE These sentences have comma splices. Correct them in two ways. Follow the example.

1. Abdullah went to Europe, he visited many countries.

   a. *Abdullah went to Europe, and he visited many countries.*

   b. *Abdullah went to Europe. He visited many countries.*

2. I fell down the stairs yesterday, I broke my leg.

   a. _____

   b. _____

3. We wanted to have sushi for dinner, we went to our favorite Japanese restaurant.

   a. _____

   b. _____

4. Dave and his brother went on a camping trip, they didn't have a very good time.

   a. _____

   b. _____

5. William enjoys playing tennis, he also likes to play baseball.

   a. _____

   b. _____

6. I like my history class, I don't like my biology class.

   a. _____

   b. _____

7. Good drivers obey traffic signs, they do not drive over the speed limit.

   a. _____

   b. _____

8. It was raining, I brought an umbrella.

   a. _____

   b. _____

9. She works on the weekends, she works in the evenings, too.

   a. _____

   b. _____

10. Hwan left for class early, he arrived late.

   a. _____

   b. _____

WRITING PARAGRAPHS USING ORDER OF IMPORTANCE

PRACTICE A **Answer the following questions.**

1. Would you rather live in a small town or a big city? _____

2. Which do you think is more important, luck or hard work? _____

3. Would you rather work for a large company or a small company? _____

B Choose one of the questions from Exercise A to answer in a paragraph. Make a list of supporting points on the lines provided. Do not worry about the order.

Supporting Points

_____ _____

_____ _____

_____ _____

_____ _____

_____ _____

C Go over your list and cross out any items that do not belong. Then number the points in order of importance. Put a _1_ in front of the one you feel is the most important, and so on.

D Write a topic sentence for your paragraph.

_____

E Using the topic sentence and your list of supporting points, write a paragraph about your topic. You may begin with what you feel is the most important point or save it for last. Remember to use signal words. Include a title.

_____

_____

_____

_____

_____

_____

_____

_____

EQUAL ORDER PARAGRAPHS

Sometimes you may feel that all of the points you are using to support your main idea are equally important. In this case, you list your points one by one. The order that you use is not important.

  A **Read the model paragraph and answer the questions. Notice that the author gives equal importance to each point. The sentences are not in a specific order of importance.**

Protecting Yourself from the Heat

There are several ways you can protect yourself when it gets very hot outside. One way is to avoid strenuous activity until the sun goes down. In addition, it is a good idea to wear lightweight and light-colored clothing. It is also important to drink a lot of water throughout the day so you don't get dehydrated. Finally, try to stay in the shade or in air-conditioned places.

1. What is the topic sentence? _____

2. How many supporting points does the author give? _____

B **Have you ever thought about why trees are so important? Read the list of things that trees do for our planet.**

- release oxygen into the air for animals to breathe
- provide food and shelter for many animals
- give us wood for building, fuel, and many other products
- prevent soil from being washed away

1. Discuss the list above with a partner. What are some other ways trees are valuable?

2. Write one or two more reasons that trees are valuable. _____

_____

3. Complete the paragraph about the importance of trees. Use equal order.

_____

Trees are very important to life on our planet. _____

_____

_____

_____

_____

_____

USE YOUR IMAGINATION

Read the agenda Martha Dickey prepared for a conference. After she sent out the agenda, she made several changes to the schedule.

FLORIDA ADVERTISING GROUP

Spring Conference Agenda
April 25
Convention Center, Miami, Florida

Registration Deadline: ~~April 10~~ *March 30*

Time	Event	Location
7:30 ~~7:00~~–8:30 A.M.	Continental breakfast	Main Lobby
8:30–9:00 A.M.	Conference welcome and opening remarks	Grand Ballroom B
9:00–10:15 A.M.	Morning sessions	
	New Frontiers: Marketing on Social Networking Sites	Conference Room 1
	Protecting Consumer Privacy	Conference Room 3
	Competition in Online Markets	Conference Room 4
10:15–10:45 A.M.	Networking break	Main Lobby
11:00–12:00 P.M.	Keynote speaker Jason Keating	
	Fast Forward: What's Next in Online Video Advertising?	Grand Ballroom
12:00–1:00 P.M.	Lunch	Conference Center Dining Hall A
1:00–2:30 P.M.	Afternoon workshops	
	Measuring Success	*Conference Room 3* ~~Conference Room 2~~
	Web Marketing Techniques That Work	Conference Room 1
2:30–3:00 P.M.	Networking break	Main Lobby
3:00–5:00 P.M.	Exhibitors display	Second Floor Lobby
5:00–6:00 P.M.	Closing remarks	Grand Ballroom
7:30–10:00 ~~7:00–9:30~~ P.M.	Dinner	Sophie's Restaurant

1. Circle the changes Martha made to the agenda.

2. Martha needs to send an email to her colleagues to notify them of the changes. Imagine you are Martha and write an email that explains the changes to the schedule. Use signal words to introduce each change. Remember that email messages are usually short and to the point.

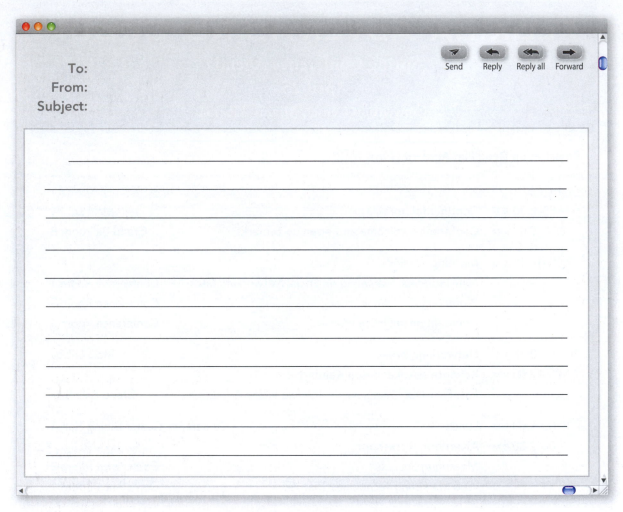

PUTTING IT ALL TOGETHER

Choose one of the following topics to write about.

- tips for staying healthy
- ways to impress your date
- things you like to do on the weekend
- qualities of a good friend

1. Make a list of ideas to support the topic. Do not worry about the order.

2. Go over your list and cross out any items that do not belong because they do not support the topic.

3. Write a topic sentence for your paragraph.

_____

4. Use the topic sentence and your list of supporting points to write a paragraph. You may put your supporting details in any order you choose. Remember to use signal words. Include a title.

_____

_____

_____

_____

_____

_____

YOU BE THE EDITOR

Read the paragraph. It contains eleven mistakes. Correct the mistakes. Copy the corrected paragraph on a separate piece of paper.

The Many Uses of Corn

There are several reasons why corn is one of the most important food sources in the world, it has many other important use as well. First of all, one of the most valuables uses of corn is as an alternative energy source. Ethanol, which is make from corn, is used to fuel cars and planes. some houses are even heated with ethanol fuel. Corn is also used to make plastics and fabrics. In fact, corn are used in thousands of products such as glue, shoe polish, aspirin, ink, and cosmetics. Finally, the syrup from corn sweetens Ice cream, soda, and candy. Scientists continue to researches new uses of corn, they find more every year.

ON YOUR OWN

Write a paragraph about one of the following topics.
- the qualities of a good/bad restaurant (or hotel, school, etc.)
- the qualities of a good/bad driver (or restaurant server, babysitter, taxi driver, etc.)
- your favorite reality show on TV
- your favorite smartphone app

When you describe a place, such as a room or a park, you organize the details according to their location. This is called *spatial order*. The easiest way to do this is to choose a starting point. Then describe where things are located in relation to your starting point. Decide on a logical method to follow, such as left to right, top to bottom, or front to back.

SPATIAL ORDER ORGANIZATION

Read the model paragraph. Put a check (✔) below the picture that the paragraph describes.

My Office

My home office is not very big, but it is comfortable. The light blue walls are calming. There are big windows on the left wall, so the room is sunny and cheerful. I hung a tapestry from Thailand between the windows. My old oak desk fits perfectly under the two big windows. When I work at my desk, I can look out the window. I have a wonderful view of the woods in back of my house. There is a small red sofa on the back wall where my cat loves to take a nap. There is a bookcase on the right side of the sofa and a file cabinet on the left side. There are several maps of places I have visited hanging on the wall to the right. Under the maps, I have a long narrow table with pictures of my family and friends on the top. The floor in the middle of the room is covered with a beautiful handmade Turkish rug. It has a floral design. I really enjoy working in my office.

Topic Sentences for Spatial Order Paragraphs

A spatial order paragraph must have a good topic sentence. The topic sentence is the first sentence. It should include the topic (the name of the place) and the controlling idea (something about the place). Look at these examples:

- **My back porch** is a **great place to relax**.
- **My attic** is **crowded and disorganized**.

PRACTICE **Write a topic sentence for each paragraph.**

1.

My Favorite Room

My bedroom is my favorite room in our house. When you walk into the room, you will notice the large sliding glass doors to the left that open onto a balcony. My bed is opposite the balcony, on the wall to the right. From my bed, I have a beautiful view of the garden. There is a painting above my bed that my great aunt painted. I have a beautiful antique nightstand next to my bed on the right. On the back wall, there is a comfortable chair where I sit and read. Next to the chair is a small table that is always covered with magazines. I love to spend time in my bedroom.

2.

My Organized Desk

_____ My laptop computer is in the center where it is easy for me to reach. To the left of the computer, I keep a basket with pens and pencils. My calendar is next to the basket. There is a small desk lamp in the right corner and a picture of my son next to it. It's easy to work at my desk because everything is in its place.

3.

My Messy Desk

_____ In the center of the desk is a pile of old magazines. The pile keeps growing. Next to that, there are dirty coffee cups and a can of soda. There is a lamp in the left corner, but I use it to hold some baseball caps. An old box is on the right side of the desk. Inside the box are my bills, important papers, and receipts. The box is getting so full that soon the top won't fit. I really should organize my desk soon.

4.

An International Museum

_____ When you walk in the main entrance, the American art is on the first floor on your left. The Asian collection is directly in front of you, and the Islamic art is on your right. European paintings and sculptures are on the left side of the museum on the second floor. The Egyptian mummies and statues are on the opposite side of the museum on the second floor. The Greek and Roman statues are on the left side of the third floor. There is a carved Chinese bench between the statues. Finally, the African collection is on the right side. When you leave the museum, you feel like you've seen something from almost every part of the world.

5.

A Beautiful Lobby

_____ As you walk up the central grand staircase that leads to the first-floor lobby, you will feel enchanted. The whole lobby has beautiful, thick, red carpeting and wood paneled walls. In the center of the lobby, there is an exquisite crystal chandelier hanging from the ceiling. Under that sits a large, round, antique table with a vase full of fresh flowers. Around the table there are a few elegant, but comfortable, leather sofas and chairs for people to relax in. To the right of the table, there is piano. There are more chairs and small tables behind the piano in an area that opens onto a lovely garden outside. A local musician plays soft jazz for the guests having afternoon tea. On the right side of the lobby is a long desk. Behind the desk, there are usually several people checking people in and out of the hotel. Finally, in the back of the lobby across from the front desk, there is a small gift shop.

GRAMMAR FOR WRITING: Prepositions of Place

Prepositions of place, such as **on**, **under**, and **in**, are often used as signal words to show position or location.

Study the chart.

PREPOSITIONS OF PLACE

above	beside	next to	opposite
across	between	on	outside
around	in	on both sides	over
at	in (the) back of	on the bottom	to the east (west, north, south)
at the bottom	in (the) front of	on the end	to the left (right)
at the end	in the center	on the left (side)	under
at the top	in the middle	on the right (side)	
behind	inside	on (the) top of	

PRACTICE **A** Underline the prepositions of place in the paragraphs on pages 63 and 64.

B Study the floor plan of Lourie's Department Store. Then read the paragraph that follows. Notice that the paragraph is organized by spatial order. Underline the prepositions of place.

LOURIE'S FIRST FLOOR

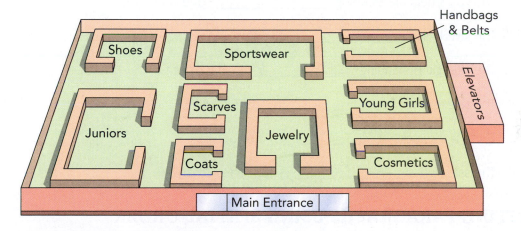

The first floor of Lourie's sells clothing and accessories for women. As you enter the store through the main entrance, the jewelry department is directly in front of you in the middle of the store. The coat department is on the left and the cosmetics department is on the right. The juniors' shop is on the left, next to coats. Women's shoes are located in the back left corner. Next to the shoe department, behind jewelry, is the sportswear department. Handbags and belts are next to sportswear in the back right corner. The young girls' department is on the right, between handbags and cosmetics. The elevators are on the right wall.

C Look at the picture of the jewelry department and complete the following sentences with the correct prepositions.

1. The customers are standing _____ the counter.

2. The jewelry is _____ the case.

3. The little girl is standing _____ her parents.

4. The saleswoman is _____ the counter.

5. There is a mirror _____ the counter.

6. The sale sign is _____ the saleswoman.

WRITING PARAGRAPHS USING SPATIAL ORDER

Begin spatial order paragraphs with a topic sentence that tells you the name of the place and something about it. Include supporting sentences that give details that describe the place. End with a concluding sentence that gives a final thought about the place.

WRITER'S TIP: Organizing Details

There are several ways to organize the details in a spatial order paragraph. For example, you may start on the left side and move right, go from right to left, or from top to bottom. Choose the pattern that best suits your topic, and then stick to that pattern throughout the paragraph.

A **Complete the floor plan of the second floor of Lourie's using the information in the sentences.**

LOURIE'S SECOND FLOOR

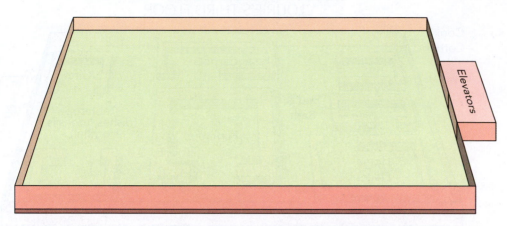

1. When you get off the elevator, the men's casual clothing department is to the left.

2. Men's shoes are to the right of the elevator.

3. The coat and suit department are straight ahead in the middle of the store.

4. Shirts and sweaters are behind the coat and suit department in the left corner.

5. The ties are in the right corner, next to the shirts and sweaters.

B **Complete the paragraph describing the second floor. Use spatial order to organize the information. Think about the pattern that best suits your paragraph: left to right, right to left, bottom to top, top to bottom.**

The second floor of Lourie's has all the clothing a man needs. When you get off the

elevator, _____

_____

_____

_____

_____

_____

_____

_____

_____

C Write a paragraph describing the third floor based on the following floor plan. Use spatial order to organize the information. Think about the pattern that best suits your paragraph: left to right, right to left, bottom to top, top to bottom. Begin with a topic sentence.

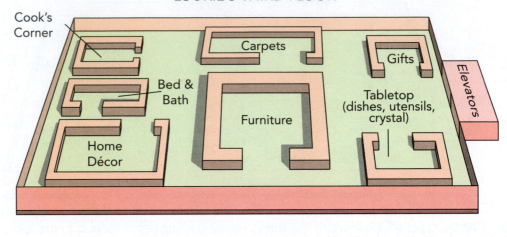

LOURIE'S THIRD FLOOR

Cook's Corner
Carpets
Gifts
Bed & Bath
Tabletop (dishes, utensils, crystal)
Furniture
Home Décor
Elevators

_____

_____

_____

_____

_____

_____

_____

PUTTING IT ALL TOGETHER

Follow the steps to draw a simple picture of one of the following: a room in your house, apartment, or dormitory; a hotel room; your office or classroom.

1. Make a list of the things in the room such as furniture, lights, rugs, artwork, and windows.

_____   _____

_____   _____

_____   _____

_____   _____

_____   _____

2. On a separate piece of paper, draw a picture of the room including the items on your list.

3. Write a paragraph describing the room. Use spatial order to organize your information. Think about the pattern that best suits your paragraph: left to right, right to left, bottom to top, top to bottom.

_____

_____

_____

_____

_____

4. After you have written your paragraph, find a partner. Ask your partner to read your paragraph and draw a picture of the room based on your description. Don't show your partner your picture.

5. Compare your picture and your partner's picture of the room. Are there any differences? If yes, discuss them with your partner. Can you think of ways to make your description clearer? Revise your paragraph on a separate piece of paper.

USE YOUR IMAGINATION

Imagine that your school is putting on a production of a play you wrote. You need to write a description of the scenery you want on the stage. Draw a picture of the scenery. Use the picture to write a description of the set.

_____

_____

_____

_____

_____

JUST FOR FUN

Use the map of the United States to complete the paragraph that follows.

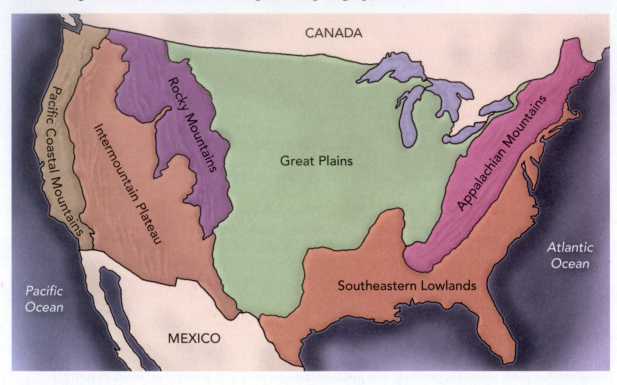

The United States is a large country in North America bordered by Canada to the north and

Mexico to the south. The Atlantic Ocean lies to the east and the Pacific Ocean lies to the west. The

United States has six very different regions. _____

_____

_____

_____

_____

_____

_____

_____

_____

_____

_____

_____

Read the following paragraph. It contains eight mistakes. Correct the mistakes. Copy the corrected paragraph on a separate piece of paper.

My Bright, Sunny Kitchen

I love to spend time my kitchen. It is big, sunny room with white walls and a grey tile floor. When you enter the kitchen, there is a small desk to the left. Above the desk, I have a bookshelf with my cookbooks. The dishwasher is next to the desk of the right. The refrigerator and oven are along the back wall, so there is a long grey and white marble counter between them. The microwave is at one end of that counter and the toaster oven and coffee maker are at the other end. the sink is in the middle of the counter. There is a window above the sink, and lots of cabinets on each side of the window and below the sink. In the middle of the room, i have a round table with four chair. I have a vase with flowers at the middle of the table. On the wall, in the left of the door is a pantry with food and spices.

ON YOUR OWN

Use spatial order to write a paragraph about one of the following places.

- a doctor's office
- a garden
- the view out your window
- a student lounge
- your kitchen
- your favorite place to work or study

LEARNING OUTCOME **Paragraph Writing:** Write a paragraph using the three steps of the writing process

Even the best writers rarely sit down and compose a perfect piece of writing on the first try. They understand that writing is a process. In this chapter, you will practice the basic steps in the writing process.

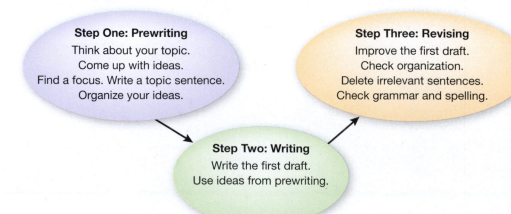

"It's not a great mission statement, but we'll revise it if things get better."

THE WRITING PROCESS

Writing is a process that involves several steps: prewriting, writing, and revising.

Step One: Prewriting
Think about your topic.
Come up with ideas.
Find a focus. Write a topic sentence.
Organize your ideas.

Step Two: Writing
Write the first draft.
Use ideas from prewriting.

Step Three: Revising
Improve the first draft.
Check organization.
Delete irrelevant sentences.
Check grammar and spelling.

STEP ONE: PREWRITING

Prewriting is the thinking, talking, reading, and organizing you do before you begin to write. Prewriting is a way of warming up your brain before you write, just as you warm up your body before you exercise. There are several ways to warm up before you write.

Brainstorming

Brainstorming is a quick way to generate a lot of ideas on a topic. The purpose is to make a list of as many ideas as possible without worrying about how you will use them. Your list can include words, phrases, sentences, or even questions. Then you use your list to come up with a specific focus for a paragraph. To brainstorm, follow these steps:

1. Begin with a general topic and write as many ideas about the topic as you can in five minutes.

2. Add more items to your list by answering the questions *What, How, When, Where, Why* and *Who*.

3. Look over your list. Group similar items on the list together.

4. Look for a focus in one of the groups and write a topic sentence.

5. Cross out items that do not belong.

You can brainstorm ideas by yourself or in a group. You already did some brainstorming with your classmates in Chapter 2, when you made a list of ideas about the topic "It is difficult to learn a new language."

PRACTICE **A** **Look at the example of brainstorming about TV commercials. Group similar items together and look for a focus. Write a topic sentence. Cross out items that do not belong.**

> TV Commercials
> Favorites
> Kinds of commercials
> BORING!
> Car commercials are my favorites
> Funny ones
> See new products
> Racist and sexist
> Too many
> Interrupt the flow of shows
> Food commercials make me hungry
> Use famous people to promote products
> Annoying
> Some have good music
> Bad for kids

B Work in a small group. Choose one person to be the secretary. Pick one of the following topics to brainstorm with your group.

- friends
- travel
- education

1. Brainstorm ideas about the topic your group chose. Each member must contribute ideas to the list. The secretary should write a list of all the ideas on a separate piece of paper.

2. Read over your list. Organize your list by grouping similar ideas. Cross out items that do not belong.

3. Look for a focus and write a topic sentence for a paragraph.

4. Write your topic sentence on the board and discuss all the topic sentences as a class.

C Choose one of the following topics to brainstorm.

- jobs
- movies
- vacations

1. On your own, follow the steps for brainstorming on a separate piece of paper.

2. Share your topic sentence and ideas with your classmates.

Clustering

Clustering is another prewriting technique. It is a visual way of showing how your ideas are connected using circles and lines. When you use this technique, you draw a diagram of your ideas. To cluster, follow these steps:

1. Write your topic in the center of a blank piece of paper and draw a circle around it.

2. Write any ideas that come into your mind about the topic in circles around the main circle.

3. Connect these ideas to the center word with a line.

4. Think about each of your new ideas, and make more circles around it.

5. Repeat this process until you run out of ideas.

6. Look at your cluster diagram. You can see which ideas go together. Write a topic sentence.

Look at the example of a cluster diagram on the topic of television commercials.

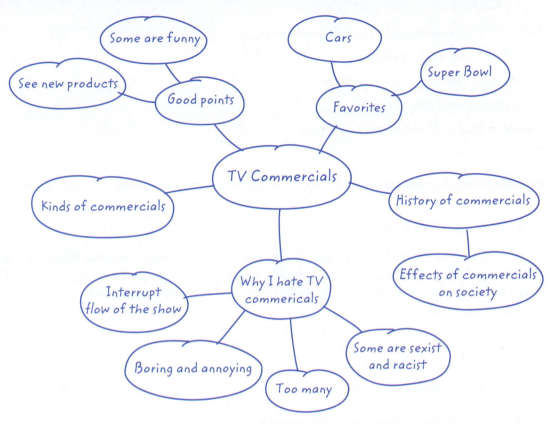

Work in a small group. Choose an aspect of TV commercials, for example *why I hate TV commercials.* (Be sure there are enough ideas to write a paragraph about this aspect.) Write a topic sentence for that paragraph. Share your topic sentence with the class.

B **Choose one of the following topics.**

- sports
- health
- music
- technology

1. Write the topic you chose in the middle of a piece of paper and follow the six steps for making a cluster diagram.

2. Look at your cluster diagram. Choose an aspect of the topic that interests you and that you have enough ideas to write a paragraph about. Write a topic sentence for that paragraph.

Organizing Your Ideas

After you have spent some time thinking about your topic and doing some prewriting exercises, you are ready to organize your information. One of the easiest ways to organize your ideas is to make a simple *list* or *outline*. Put the ideas in the order that you plan to use when you write. You can use the list or outline as a guide while you are writing. Remember that the list or outline is not permanent. You may discover new ideas or discard some ideas as you are writing.

Look at the following example of a simple outline.

> I dislike TV commercials for several reasons.
> 1. are too long and boring
> 2. interrupt the flow of the show
> 3. are racist and sexist
> 4. have a bad influence on children

On a separate sheet of paper, write a simple outline based on your brainstorming or cluster.

 ## STEP TWO: WRITING

Now you are ready to try to write the first draft of your paragraph. Remember that the first draft is not a perfect piece of writing. You can improve it before you write your final copy. When you write the first draft of your paragraph, use the ideas you generated from your prewriting. It will be helpful to use your outline or list as you write.

> **WRITER'S TIP:** Writing the First Draft
>
> When you write the first draft
>
> - begin with a topic sentence that states the main idea.
>
> - include several sentences that support the main idea.
>
> - stick to the topic—do not include information that does not support the main idea.
>
> - organize the sentences so that the order of ideas makes sense.
>
> - use signal words to help the reader understand how the ideas in your paragraph are connected.
>
> - end with a concluding sentence if appropriate.
>
> - add a title.

PRACTICE **Practice writing the first draft of a paragraph. Choose one of the topics you used in the brainstorming or clustering activity. Include a title.**

_____

_____

_____

_____

_____

_____

_____

_____

_____

_____

_____

_____

 ## STEP THREE: REVISING

Do not think of the first draft as a final product. After you write the first draft, you should look for ways to improve it. This is called *revising*. When you revise, you can add new ideas to support the topic. You can also delete irrelevant sentences. If the supporting sentences are not in a logical order, you should rearrange them. Finally, you should check your paragraph for any mistakes in grammar, punctuation, and spelling. Use a revising checklist to help you improve your paragraph.

REVISING CHECKLIST		
	YES	NO
1. Does the topic sentence include a topic and a controlling idea? If no, add one.		
2. Do all of the supporting sentences relate to the main idea? If no, cross out the sentences that do not relate.		
3. Are the sentences in the right order? If no, reorder the sentences.		
4. Is there enough support for the topic sentence? If no, add supporting sentences.		
5. Is there a title? If no, add one.		
6. Are there signal words to help guide the reader? If no, add signal words.		
7. Is the punctuation, spelling, and grammar correct? If incorrect, correct the errors.		

Work in a small group. Read the paragraphs. Use the Revising Checklist to help you revise the paragraphs. Discuss where you would add the highlighted sentence to the paragraph. Draw an asterisk (*) where it should be inserted. Write the revised paragraph on the lines or on a separate piece of paper.

1.

An Annoying Brother

My little brother, Tim, has several annoying habits. For one thing, he follows me everywhere. He is like my shadow. I enjoy my privacy, but because of Tim, I am never alone. His most annoying habit is eating with his mouth open. I feel sick when I have lunch with him. I hope he learns some table manners soon. Tim has curly red hair, just like me. Another problem is that Tim leaves his toys all over the house. I am always tripping on his toy cars or trucks. The house is always a mess with Tim around.

==He even follows me into the bathroom.==

_____

_____

_____

_____

_____

_____

2.

Our Annual Talent Show

Every year, my school has a talent show to raise money for new books for the library. This year, I was the host. The show was amazing and everyone involved did a great job. One group of students formed a band and played three popular songs. My favorite act, however, was definitely my friend Ben's magic show. Ben is also a good student. He did about ten tricks that no one in the audience could figure out. There were also some nice dance performances and a comedy act that left the audience crying from laughing so much. With the help of all the great performers and, of course, the audience who came to see the show, we raised close to $5,000.

==That can buy a lot of new books!==

B On your own, read the paragraphs. Use the Revising Checklist on page 77 to help you revise the paragraphs. Discuss where you would add the highlighted sentence to the paragraph. Draw an asterisk (*) where it should be inserted. Write the revised paragraph on the lines.

1.

Korean Food Chain Serves Healthy Choices

Some fast-food restaurants from Asia are serving diners with a healthier alternative to the usual choices of burgers and fries. For example, a Korean food chain, Sorabol, is bringing traditional Korean cuisine to fast-food venues in the United States. Unlike most American fast-food that is pre-made and then delivered to the store, Sorabol's food is prepared every day, so you know the ingredients are fresh. Lots of fast-food restaurants offer many kinds of pizza. Sorabol is a family-owned chain, and the owners pride themselves on offering a clean, casual, inexpensive dining experience to fit today's fast-paced society. With restaurants already established in West Coast cities such as San Francisco and Seattle, Sorabol is planning on expanding across the country as its popularity increases. Hopefully, we can all enjoy Korean BBQ take-out over the next couple of years!

In fact, plans are already underway to expand to Washington, D.C., and New York City.

2.

> ### My Book Club
>
> My friends and I love to read so much that we started our own book club. At the beginning of each month, one member of the club selects a book for us to read. That person sends an email to everyone with the title and author of the book. She is also responsible for hosting a small party on the last Monday of each month when we all get together to have dinner and discuss the book. The person who chooses the book changes each month, which is great because I get to read and discuss all different types of books. For example, last month we read a mystery my friend Beth recommended. I met Beth last year at work. This month, we are reading a biography of Abraham Lincoln. Next month, it's my turn to pick a book. Book clubs are a great way to keep reading and do something fun with your friends.
>
> ==I'll probably pick a romance novel by Marianne Lewis, my favorite author.==

_____

_____

_____

_____

_____

_____

_____

_____

GRAMMAR FOR WRITING: Sentence Fragments

Every English sentence must have a subject and a verb. It must also express a complete thought. If a sentence lacks a subject or a verb or is not a complete thought, it is called a *fragment*. Check your writing to make sure you do not have any sentence fragments.

There are three common kinds of fragments. Study the chart.

PROBLEM	EXAMPLES/SOLUTIONS
no subject	*Fragment:* Wrote a paragraph about friendship. *Complete sentence:* **Allie** wrote a paragraph about friendship.
no verb	*Fragment:* The whole team, as well as the fans. *Complete sentence:* The whole team, as well as the fans, **ran onto the field**.
not a complete thought	*Fragment:* As soon as I fell asleep. *Complete sentence:* As soon as I fell asleep, **the phone rang**.

PRACTICE **A** **Read these fragments. Add a subject to make them a complete sentence.**

1. Walked to the store to buy some fruit.

   _____

2. Were too tired to watch the movie tonight.

   _____

3. Usually gets up early, so he can exercise before work.

   _____

5. Was late for her dentist appointment.

   _____

6. Am sorry you are having trouble meeting people.

   _____

B **Read these fragments. Add a verb to make them a complete sentence.**

1. Jane to a new apartment last week.

   _____

2. We usually the bus to school.

   _____

3. The plane two hours late.

   _____

4. Hasan English classes at the local community college.

   _____

5. My roommate the funniest person I know.

_____

6. The book difficult to understand.

_____

C **Read these fragments. Add information to make them a complete thought.**

1. Before it starts to rain.

_____

2. Because I didn't study enough.

_____

3. After we finish dinner.

_____

4. At the art museum right now.

_____

5. As soon as she sent the email.

_____

6. When I got home after a long day at work.

_____

D **Write *C* in front of each complete sentence. Write *F* in front of each sentence fragment. Then rewrite the fragments so that they are complete sentences.**

__F__ 1. After I got home from a long day at the office.

After I got home from a long day at the office, I was too tired to

make dinner.

_____ 2. Mr. Steven's older brother and sister.

_____

_____ 3. The roads are slippery from the rain, so drive carefully and keep your lights on.

_____

_____ 4. Under the table where the cat usually hides.

_____

_____ 5. To apply for a scholarship at the University of Pennsylvania.

_____

_____ 6. Two young men from different cities met on a train going to Paris.

_____

_____ 7. Because I knew it would be too expensive to fly there.

_____

_____ 8. Has been painted several times over the years.

_____

PRACTICING THE STEPS OF THE WRITING PROCESS

Paragraph Practice 1

Read the situation and follow the steps of the writing process.

Your friend has just moved to a new place and is having trouble meeting new people. You are writing your friend a note of encouragement. You want to give some tips about how to make new friends.

Prewriting

A **Brainstorm a list or make a cluster diagram of ideas about how to make new friends. Use a separate piece of paper.**

B **Share your ideas with a partner. Add some new ideas. Cross out any ideas that are not related to the main idea.**

C **Write a topic sentence.**

_____

Writing

Write the first draft of your paragraph. Use your prewriting as a guide. Begin with your topic sentence and organize your sentences in a logical order. Include a title.

_____

_____

_____

_____

_____

_____

🔍 Revising

Ⓐ **Read your paragraph. Try to improve it. Use the Revising Checklist on page 77.**

_____

_____

_____

_____

_____

_____

_____

_____

Ⓑ **Copy your revised paragraph on a separate piece of paper.**

Paragraph Practice 2

Read the situation and follow the steps of the writing process. Complete the steps with a partner.

You are writing an article about international students for your local newspaper. You want to include a paragraph about your partner.

💡 Prewriting

Ⓐ **Ask and answer the questions with a partner. Write your partner's answers on the lines.**

Your partner's name: _____

1. Where are you from? _____

2. What is your native language? _____

3. Do you know any other languages? _____

4. Why are you learning English? _____

_____

5. Have you visited any other countries? If so, which ones? _____

_____

B Write three more questions to ask your partner. You can ask questions about the following:

- job/education
- hobbies
- family

Write your partner's answers.

1. Question: _____

   Answer: _____

2. Question: _____

   Answer: _____

3. Question: _____

   Answer: _____

C Write a topic sentence about your partner.

_____

Writing

Write the first draft of a paragraph about your partner. Use the information from your partner's answers as a guide.

_____

_____

_____

_____

_____

Revising

A Ask your partner to read your paragraph. Does your partner have any suggestions? If so, write them down. You can also use the Revising Checklist on page 77 to help you.

_____

_____

_____

_____

B Copy your revised paragraph on a separate piece of paper.

YOU BE THE EDITOR

Read the paragraph. It contains ten mistakes. Correct the mistakes. Copy the corrected paragraph on a separate piece of paper.

How to improve Your Performance on an Exam

There are several thing you can do to improve your performance on an exam. First, should get a good night's sleep the night before the test. that means sleeping for at least eight hour. It is also important to eat a good breakfast on the morning of the exam, you won't have hungry during the exam Finally, to bring a bottle of water to the test in case you got thirsty. Just don't drink too much, or you may have to get up in the middle of the exam for a bathroom break.

ON YOUR OWN

Choose one of the topics in this chapter that you did not already write about. Write a paragraph on the topic. Practice the steps of prewriting, writing, and revising. Remember to use the Revising Checklist on page 77.

CHAPTER 7 › Supporting the Main Idea

Supporting the Main Idea

LEARNING OUTCOME

Paragraph Writing: Write a paragraph using charts, graphs and quotes to support the main idea

You have learned that a paragraph is a group of sentences about one main idea that is stated in a topic sentence. You have also learned that a paragraph needs supporting sentences to develop the main idea. Many paragraphs have three major supporting sentences. Support can come from many places, such as your own personal experience, examples, quotes, or facts. In this chapter, you will learn more about how to support a main idea.

ADDING ADDITIONAL DETAILS

As you begin to write longer, more developed paragraphs, you will need to add details to your main supporting points. This will make your paragraphs more complete. A paragraph is complete when all of the supporting sentences and additional details sufficiently prove your main idea. If there are not enough supporting sentences and details to prove your main idea, then the paragraph is incomplete. In that case, you need to add more information.

Read the model paragraph about reducing stress. It has a topic sentence, three supporting sentences, and a concluding sentence.

> ### Reducing Stress
>
> I do several things to reduce my stress during final exams. First of all, I exercise every day. In addition, I am more careful about my diet. Finally, I take breaks while I am studying. All of these things help me through the stressful week of finals.

Read this revised model paragraph. Now, each major supporting point is followed by additional details that provide more information.

Reducing Stress

I do several things to reduce my stress during final exams. First of all, I exercise every day. I try to do at least thirty minutes of aerobic exercise such as riding my bike or jogging. Exercising helps me focus on something else, and it makes me feel better. In addition, I am more careful about my diet during finals. I avoid foods that are high in sugar because they make me jittery, and I stay away from fatty foods because they make me tired. I try to eat well-balanced meals and healthy snacks such as fruit and nuts. Finally, I take breaks while I am studying. Every few hours, I do something enjoyable such as watch my favorite TV show, call my friends, or listen to music. I relax during my breaks and feel more energized when I go back to studying. All of these things help me through the stressful week of finals.

PRACTICE **A** **Complete the simple outline based on the paragraph you've just read.**

Topic sentence: I do several things to reduce my stress during final exams.

Main supporting point 1: *I exercise every day.*

Detail: *I do thirty minutes of aerobic exercise such as riding my bike or jogging.*

Detail: _____

Main supporting point 2: _____

Detail: _____

Detail: _____

Main supporting point 3: _____

Detail: _____

Detail: _____

B **Make this paragraph more complete by adding specific details to each main supporting point.**

There are several ways to save money on your monthly expenses. First of all, you can spend less money on food. _____

_____

You can also economize on entertainment. _____

_____

Finally, you can save money on rent. _____

_____

USING EXAMPLES FOR SUPPORT

Writers often use examples to support topic sentences and main supporting points. In fact, examples are one of the best ways to help readers understand your ideas.

Read the model paragraph. Underline the examples.

An Enthusiastic Collector

My cousin Alex loves to collect things. For example, he has an amazing stamp collection. He started collecting stamps about ten years ago and now he has some very rare and valuable ones. He keeps all of his stamps neatly arranged in special leather albums. Alex also collects coins from all around

the world. He recently told me he has coins from more than 100 countries. In addition, Alex collects some more unusual things such as antique toys and old model airplanes. He arranges them in display cases around his apartment. According to Alex, collecting things can be very educational. For instance, he has learned a lot about the history of certain places in the process of collecting stamps and coins. Last but not least, Alex seems to collect people. I have never met anyone with so many friends.

GRAMMAR FOR WRITING: *For Example, For Instance, Such As*

The phrases *for example* and *for instance* are used at the beginning of a complete sentence to introduce examples. Use a comma (,) after the phrase. The phrase *such as* is used to introduce short examples within a sentence. Commas are usually not necessary.

PHRASE	EXAMPLES
for example	Martha enjoys outdoor sports. **For example,** she loves snowboarding and skiing.
for instance	My computer has lots of problems. **For instance,** it freezes almost once a day.
such as	I prefer to wear clothes made out of natural fibers **such as** cotton, silk, and wool.

Read each statement. Then choose an example from the box to support each statement. Write the appropriate example on the lines following the statement. Remember to begin the example with the phrase *for example* or *for instance* and to use a comma.

1. Are you bored with your job? If so, there are plenty of unusual jobs to help make working

   more pleasurable for you. _____

   _____

2. Some people believe that dreams can indicate future events. _____

   _____

3. In addition to shoes that make a fashion statement, there are many different kinds of shoes

   for special purposes. _____

   _____

- There are special shoes for playing soccer, tap dancing, hiking, and bowling.
- A furniture tester actually gets paid to sit in chairs and sofas and make sure the furniture is comfortable before it is sold to the public.
- In some cultures, a dream of a rainbow is believed to predict good fortune.

B **Complete the sentences.**

1. Some colors, such as _____ and _____, have a soothing effect on me.

2. Games, such as _____ and _____, are fun to watch.

3. Exercises, such as _____ and _____, are good for your heart.

4. Some of my friends, such as _____ and _____, are good listeners.

5. Several planets, such as _____ and _____, have at least one moon.

WRITING PARAGRAPHS WITH EXAMPLES

Paragraph Practice 1

 Prewriting

A Work in a group. Look at the paragraph *An Enthusiastic Collector* on page 89. Discuss what details are used to help support the examples and make them clear.

B Write two or three examples for each statement. Then discuss your examples in a small group.

1. Several inventions have dramatically changed the way people live.

   _____

   _____

2. In my culture, there are certain things that are considered impolite.

   _____

   _____

3. Recycling is an important, but easy, way to help the planet.

   _____

   _____

C Choose one of the statements in exercise B to use as a topic sentence for a paragraph. Use your examples as the main supporting points. Add details to strengthen these points. Make a simple outline before you write.

Topic sentence: _____

Main supporting point 1: _____

Detail: _____

Detail: _____

Main supporting point 2: _____

Detail: _____

Detail: _____

Main supporting point 3: _____

Detail: _____

Detail: _____

 **Writing**

Write your first draft. Use your outline to help you. Use the expressions *for example, for instance,* and *such as.* Add a title.

_____

_____

_____

_____

_____

_____

_____

_____

_____

_____

_____

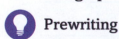 **Revising**

A **Look for ways to improve your paragraph. Use the Revising Checklist on page 77. Also think about these questions as you revise your paragraph.**

1. Are all of your examples relevant? In other words, does each example relate to the main point it is supporting?

2. Did you add details for the main supporting points?

3. Did you use the expressions *for example, for instance,* and *such as* correctly?

B **Revise your paragraph on a separate piece of paper.**

Paragraph Practice 2

Prewriting

A **People learn in different ways. Some people learn by reading about things. Other people learn by doing things. Still others learn by listening to people talk about things. Discuss these learning styles in small groups.**

B **Think about the different ways people learn. Which of these ways is most effective for you?**

C Make a list of examples that support your answer.

_____   _____

_____   _____

_____   _____

_____   _____

D On a separate piece of paper, make an outline before you begin to write a first draft.

✒ Writing

Write the first draft of a paragraph about how you learn new information best. Use your outline and specific examples to support your idea. Add a title.

_____

_____

_____

_____

_____

_____

_____

_____

_____

_____

_____

_____

🔍 Revising

A Exchange papers with a partner. Look for ways to improve your partner's paragraph. Use the Revising Checklist on page 77. Do the examples support the topic sentence? Give your partner some advice.

B Read the suggestions your partner gave you. Decide which of these suggestions you will use. Make your changes. Write your revised paragraph on a separate piece of paper.

Follow-up Activity

A Interview each of your classmates. Find out what way each of them learns best. Then complete the chart about learning styles in your class.

Learning Style	Number of People
Learn best by reading about things	
Learn best by doing things	
Learn best by listening to people talk about things	

B Write a paragraph about the different learning styles in your class.

Paragraph Practice 3

Prewriting

A Many things influence young adults. Which do you think has more influence—family, friends, or media? Discuss this with your classmates.

B Find several people who agree with you. On a separate sheet of paper, make a list of examples to support your idea.

Writing

Work together to write a paragraph. Use your examples. Add a title.

_____

 **Revising**

A **Look for ways to improve your group's paragraph.**

    1. Are all of your examples relevant?

    2. Can you add any more examples?

B **Check for errors in grammar, spelling, and punctuation. Revise your group's paragraph on a separate piece of paper.**

Follow-up Activity

Find a group that has a different position and exchange paragraphs. Read each other's paragraphs and discuss the question again. Do you still have the same opinion?

USING A PERSONAL EXPERIENCE FOR SUPPORT

Writing about a personal experience is another effective way to support a topic sentence.

Read the paragraph. Then discuss the questions with a partner.

Stranger or Friend?

Sometimes a stranger can be a real friend. The woman I met on my way home from work yesterday is a perfect example. I left my office late and forgot that my car needed gas. I had been driving on the expressway for about ten minutes when the car started making strange noises. Then it suddenly stopped. I was out of gas, and I was scared because it was getting dark. After a few minutes, a young couple stopped and offered to help me. They went to a gas station, bought a big can of gas, and put the gas in my tank. The woman told me that when she saw me looking so alone and upset, she told her husband to stop. She wanted to help me because she hoped that someone would stop and help her in a similar situation.

1. What is the topic sentence?

2. How are the supporting sentences organized? What signal words help the organization?

3. What is the concluding sentence?

4. Do you think the student's experience supports her topic sentence? How?

Paragraph Practice 1

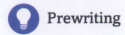 Prewriting

A **Discuss these expressions with your teacher and classmates. What do they mean?**

- The love of money is the root of all evil.
- Two heads are better than one.
- Variety is the spice of life.
- Haste makes waste.
- Don't count your chickens before they hatch.
- Too many cooks spoil the broth.

B **Choose one expression to write about. Think of an experience from your own life that proves or disproves the expression. Tell a partner about your experience.**

 Writing

Complete the paragraph with a personal experience. Organize your ideas according to time order. Use the signal words in Chapter 3 to connect your ideas. Add a title.

_____

    The expression, "_____"

(is usually / is not always) true. _____

_____

_____

_____

_____

_____

_____

 Revising

A **Read over the paragraph you wrote. Look for ways to improve it. Use the Revising Checklist on page 77 to help you. As you revise, think about these questions.**

1. Are the sentences in correct time order?

2. Did you include signal words?

3. Did you include a concluding sentence?

B **Write your revised paragraph on a separate piece of paper.**

Paragraph Practice 2

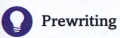

Prewriting

A **Discuss these statements in a small group.**

- Good things happen when you least expect them.
- Sometimes hard work is not rewarded.
- Things don't often turn out the way you planned.

B **Think of an experience in your life that supports one of the statements. Make a list of the events in your experience. Use time order.**

_____   _____

_____   _____

_____   _____

C **Write a topic sentence for your paragraph.**

_____

Writing

Use your list to write the first draft of the paragraph supporting the statement you chose. Add a title.

_____

_____

_____

_____

_____

_____

_____

_____

_____

_____

 **Revising**

A Read the paragraph you wrote. Look for ways to improve it. Use the Revising Checklist on page 77 to help you.

B Write your revised paragraph on a separate piece of paper.

USING FACTS AND STATISTICS FOR SUPPORT

Writers often use facts and statistics to support their main idea. A fact is something you know to be true because it exists, has happened, or can be proven. Statistics are facts presented as numbers.

Read the paragraph a student wrote. Work with a partner. Discuss the facts and statistics that support the main idea.

> ### A Ride on the Trans-Siberian Railroad
>
> Last summer, I rode the Trans-Siberian Railroad, the longest continuous rail line in the world. It actually crosses the whole Russian Federation. I boarded the train in the capital, Moscow, and rode 5,870 miles (9,446 kilometers) to the Pacific port of Vladivostok. It was a long ride, but I wasn't bored at all. The whole journey took eight days to complete. During that time, I met lots of interesting people. We crossed eight time zones along the way. It was a long trip, but well worth it.

PRACTICE A Read the news article. Notice the facts and statistics that support the main idea. Discuss them in a small group.

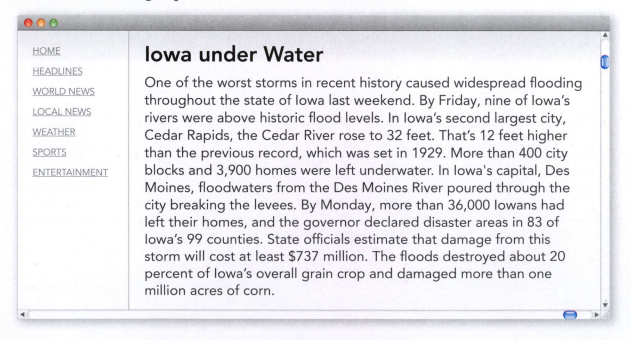

HOME
HEADLINES
WORLD NEWS
LOCAL NEWS
WEATHER
SPORTS
ENTERTAINMENT

Iowa under Water

One of the worst storms in recent history caused widespread flooding throughout the state of Iowa last weekend. By Friday, nine of Iowa's rivers were above historic flood levels. In Iowa's second largest city, Cedar Rapids, the Cedar River rose to 32 feet. That's 12 feet higher than the previous record, which was set in 1929. More than 400 city blocks and 3,900 homes were left underwater. In Iowa's capital, Des Moines, floodwaters from the Des Moines River poured through the city breaking the levees. By Monday, more than 36,000 Iowans had left their homes, and the governor declared disaster areas in 83 of Iowa's 99 counties. State officials estimate that damage from this storm will cost at least $737 million. The floods destroyed about 20 percent of Iowa's overall grain crop and damaged more than one million acres of corn.

B Read the paragraph from a brochure about the Great Smoky Mountains National Park. Underline the statistics that support the main idea.

The Great Smoky Mountains National Park is the home of a huge variety of plant and animal life. For example, there are more than 10,000 species of plants—including 130 different kinds of trees—growing in the park. That is more than in any other North American national park. There are also 1,600 flowering plant species and at least 4,000 species of non-flowering plants that live in the park. In addition, more than 200 types of birds, 66 types of mammals, and 50 native fish species make their home in the Great Smoky Mountains National Park. Another interesting fact is that more species of salamanders can be found there than anywhere else on our planet.

Paragraph Practice 1

Prewriting

A Look at the photo of ostriches. Discuss it with a partner. Have you ever seen an ostrich?

B Read the topic sentence to a paragraph on ostriches. What do you know about ostriches? How would you support this topic sentence?

Topic sentence: Ostriches, the largest and strongest birds in the world, are unusual animals.

C Read the facts and check five that you would use to support the topic sentence.

_____ • They cannot fly, but are the fastest two-legged animal on the planet; they can run up to 40 miles (65 kilometers) an hour for 30 minutes.

_____ • They are the only birds that have 2 toes on each foot; all other birds have 3 or 4 toes.

_____ • Ostriches typically eat plants, roots, and seeds.

_____ • average height: about 8 feet (2.4 meters tall)

_____ • average weight: up to 300 pounds (136 kilograms)

_____ • Contrary to popular belief, ostriches do not bury their heads in the sand.

_____ • They have feathers like all other birds.

_____ • Females can lay from 10 to 70 eggs each year.

_____ • They lay the largest bird egg, weighing about 3 pounds (1.4 kilograms) and measuring between 6 and 8 inches (about 15–20 centimeters) long.

_____ • Wild ostriches live in the dry, hot savannas and woodlands of Africa.

 **Writing**

Write a paragraph about ostriches. Include the topic sentence and facts you discussed with your partner and the facts you checked. Include a title.

_____

_____

_____

_____

_____

_____

_____

_____

 **Revising**

A Read the paragraph you wrote. Look for ways to improve it. Use the Revising Checklist on page 77 to help you.

B Write your revised paragraph on a separate piece of paper.

WRITING ABOUT INFORMATION IN GRAPHS AND CHARTS

Facts and statistics are often presented in graphs, tables, and charts. Sometimes you will need to describe this information and use it as support. The words in the boxes will help you describe changes shown on a graph, table, or chart.

Study the words on the charts.

VERBS THAT DESCRIBE CHANGE				
climb	decrease	fall	increase	remain the same
decline	drop	fluctuate	level off	rise

ADJECTIVES AND ADVERBS DESCRIBING AMOUNT OF CHANGE			
dramatic	sharp	slightly	steady
gradual	slight	small	sudden

Look at the graph. Work with a partner. Write four sentences about the average age of men at first marriage. Then write five sentences about the average age of women at first marriage. Use a variety of words from the box.

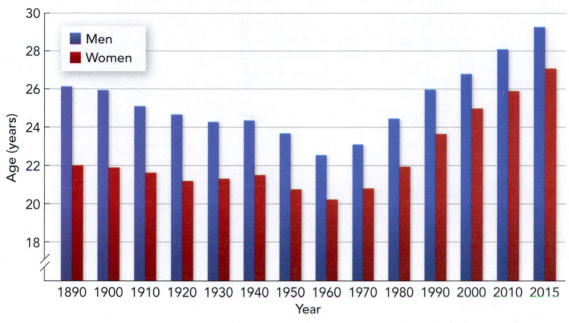

Average Age at First Marriage: 1890 to present

Men

1. <u>*The average age of men at first marriage fell between 1890 and 1950.*</u>

2. _____

3. _____

4. _____

5. _____

Women

1. _____

2. _____

3. _____

4. _____

5. _____

B Look at the graph and answer the questions that follow. The name of the graph tells you what kind of information is presented.

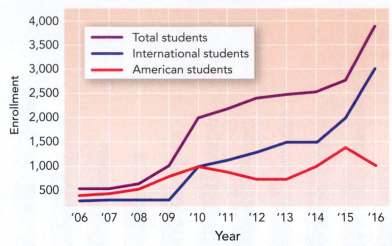

Number of Students at Springfield Academy 2006–2016

Legend: Total students, International students, American students

1. In what year was the number of international students equal to the number of American students?

_____

2. In 2016, how many international students attended Springfield Academy?

_____

3. In 2016, how many American students attended Springfield Academy?

_____

4. In what years did the number of American students remain the same?

_____

5. In what years did the number of international students remain the same?

_____

6. When did enrollment of international students reach 2000?

_____

7. In what year were there twice as many international students as American students?

_____

C **Read the situation. Think about your answers to the questions about the graph. Use the information to complete the description of the student body.**

Situation: You are an international student at Springfield Academy, and you feel that there should be more social and cultural activities for international students. Since the number of international students is growing every year, you believe that the school has a responsibility to help them socially and culturally, as well as academically.

Since the number of international students at Springfield Academy is growing every year, the school needs to organize more social and cultural activities for us. In the past, this may not have been so important, but today things are different. In 2006, _____

_____

_____

_____

_____

_____

_____

_____

_____

_____

_____

_____

_____

Because international students now represent such a large percentage of the student body, I believe that the school has a responsibility to help us outside the classroom. For example, I would like the school to organize sightseeing tours around the city. It would also be a good idea to arrange visits with American families. I'm sure all the other international students would agree with me.

Paragraph Practice 1

Prewriting

You have researched the most popular majors of international students studying in the U.S. for a report you are writing. Based on the information you found, you made this pie chart. Look at the chart and answer the questions to help you write a report.

Percentage Distribution of International Students in U.S. by Major Fields

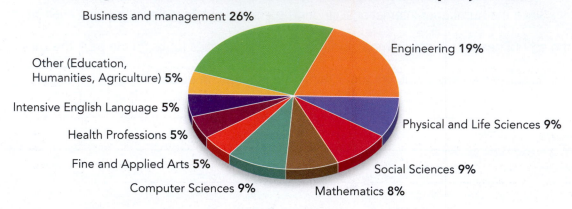

1. What is the most popular field? _____

2. What percentage of international students are studying engineering? _____

3. What is the second most popular field? _____

4. What percentage is studying business and management? _____

5. What percent of all international students is studying either engineering, or business and

   management? _____

6. What percent of all international students is studying physical and life sciences? _____

7. What percent of international students is studying social sciences? _____

8. What are some other fields that international students study? _____

   _____

Writing

Read the situation. Complete the paragraph. Support the topic sentence with facts from the chart.

Situation: You are opening an English language school. You have to write a report describing the kind of programs you will offer at your school. Based on information in the chart, you feel that the school should offer several courses in technical English.

There is a growing need to provide more technical English courses to international students. First

of all, _____

_____

_____

_____

_____

_____

_____

Revising

A   Read over your paragraph and look for ways to improve it. Use the Revising Checklist on page 77 to help you.

B   Write your revised paragraph on a separate piece of paper.

Paragraph Practice 2

Prewriting

Study the graph. It shows the amount of time it takes a typical runner to run five miles (eight kilometers) during the first eight years of running on a regular basis.

A Runner's Five-Mile Time:
The First Eight Years

1. How long does it usually take to run five miles at the end of the first year? _____

2. When does the runner achieve the greatest decrease in the amount of time it takes to run five

   miles (eight kilometers)? _____

3. How long does it take a typical runner to run five miles (eight kilometers) at the end of the second

year? _____

4. How long does it take at the end of the third year? _____

5. What happens during the following six years? _____

6. How long does it take during the seventh year? _____

7. By how many minutes does the time decrease during the first seven-year period? _____

✏️ Writing

Read the situation. Complete the letter. Support the main idea with facts from the graph.

Situation: You are writing a letter to new members of your running club. Many of the new members are discouraged because it is taking them so long to run five miles. You want to encourage them to continue running.

Dear Members,

    I know that some of you are discouraged because it is taking you so long to run five

miles. But don't give up yet. _____

_____

_____

_____

_____

_____

_____

_____

🔍 Revising

Ⓐ Read your letter and look for ways to improve it. Use the Revising Checklist on page 77 to help you.

Ⓑ Write your revised letter on a separate piece of paper.

USING QUOTES FOR SUPPORT

One of the strongest kinds of support is a quote from an expert on your topic. A *quotation*, or quote, is an exact reproduction of someone's spoken or written words. Put the quote right after the supporting sentence it relates to.

Read the model paragraph and underline the quote.

> Doctors and dieters agree that it is possible to lose weight by dieting, but the difficult part is keeping the weight off after you lose it. Research indicates that although many people successfully lose weight by going on a diet, most people gain it back within three years. If you really want to lose weight permanently, diets alone are not enough. Exercise is very important, too. According to Dr. Ian Field, "The key to permanent weight loss is getting people to change their lifestyles. Each person needs to find the right combination of diet and exercise." It's all about taking in fewer calories by eating less and burning off calories by exercising more.

GRAMMAR FOR WRITING: Punctuating Quotes

Be sure to punctuate quotes correctly. Read the rules for punctuating quotes.
- Put the person's exact words inside quotation marks ("….").
- Use a comma after the words that introduce the quote.
- Capitalize the first word of the quote.
- Place periods, commas, and question marks inside the final quotation mark.

Introducing Quotes

It is important to let your reader know that a quotation is going to follow. Here are some examples of ways to introduce a quote into your paragraph.

Examples:

Dr. Elrich states, *"Research shows that children who eat a healthy breakfast perform better at school."*

According to Dr. Elrich, *"Research shows that children who eat a healthy breakfast perform better at school."*

Study the list of common verbs used to introduce quotes.

VERBS THAT INTRODUCE QUOTES				
claim	explain	observe	say	write
comment	note	point out	state	

1. Mr. Whitnall explains it takes adults much longer than children to learn a new language

2. Dr. Jones claims sixty percent of my patients lost weight on this diet

3. Economist Marianne Watkins notes Americans spend more than $115 billion each year on fuel and electricity for their homes

4. According to Stephen Schneider even a small reduction of solar energy can affect agriculture worldwide

5. Amelia Earhart said adventure is worthwhile in itself

6. Rachel Ray said i think having an animal in your life makes you a better human

7. Dr. Ryan, director of the Canyon Zoo, observed koalas sleep 20 hours a day

8. David Miller states it is important to drink lots of water when you exercise

9. According to Samantha Bliss babies need a lot of physical contact

10. Zelda Heller points out we all need to practice ways to conserve energy

B **Work with a partner. Read each paragraph and the quote that follows. Decide where you think the quote should be inserted in the paragraph. Rewrite the paragraph on the lines provided.**

1.

Conserving Energy

High fuel prices and concern for the environment are causing many people to conserve energy. Some people are trying to save energy at home. For example, they are turning off lights and electrical appliances when they are not using them. They are also being careful about the amount of heat and air-conditioning they use. In addition, concerned people are conserving energy on the road. For instance, they are buying smaller, more fuel-efficient cars. Others are using public transportation or carpooling to save gas. Conserving energy at home and on the road are good ways to help the planet and save money.

"Set your thermostats at 75 degrees in the summer and 68 degrees in the winter to be comfortable and still save money and energy." (Gerald Christopher, Director of the Energy Conservation Center)

2.

A Dangerous Mix

Talking on a cell phone and driving do not mix. Unfortunately, too many people are combining the two activities, causing accidents that result in serious injury and death. In fact, research shows that people who use cell phones while driving are four times as likely to get into accidents that are serious enough to cause injury. Why? Using a cell phone is a big distraction. A survey of 1,200 drivers found that 73 percent talk on cell phones while driving. Cell phone use was highest among young, inexperienced drivers. It is no surprise that there has been a significant increase in the number of accidents caused by young people who were distracted while talking or texting on cell phones. These drivers were not paying attention to the road. Using cell phones while driving takes their eyes and ears off the road, and they can't give their full attention to driving. "Drivers should have both hands on the wheel and their attention focused on the road, not on a cell phone conversation. I see more and more patients every week who are in the hospital because of cell phones!" (Dr. Joel Weiss, emergency room doctor)

3.

Robo-animals

Scientists around the world are studying animal behavior in a new way by using robo-animals. Robo-animals are robots that look, smell, and act like real animals. This new technology gives scientists a better opportunity to study living things in their natural environments rather than in labs. For example, researchers in Brussels created a robotic cockroach to observe how cockroaches move around in darkness. Students and professors at the University of Amherst in Massachusetts are using a robo-squirrel to learn about the survival instincts of squirrels. Scientists in Indiana have created a robotic lizard that helps them study the mating rituals of lizards. Robo-animals are giving scientists a unique way to learn more about how animals work in groups, court, avoid danger, and communicate with each other.

"We design the robo-animals carefully so they can pass in the wild. We pay special attention to the way the robo-animals smell, move, and sound. After all, a robot's ability to blend into its natural environment is the main reason we are using them." (Marlene Standish, engineer)

_____

_____

_____

_____

_____

_____

_____

_____

_____

WRITER'S TIP: Providing Support

Remember that *supporting sentences* provide evidence to convince readers that the main idea stated in the topic sentence is true. To find supporting evidence, ask yourself: What specific details can I use to show that what I wrote in my topic sentence is true? Supporting evidence often includes reasons, examples, personal anecdotes, facts, and statistics. Choose the type of support that best proves your main point.

YOU BE THE EDITOR

Read the paragraph. It contains nine mistakes. Correct the mistakes. Copy the corrected paragraph on a separate piece of paper.

Skyscrapers on the Rise

Skyscrapers are on the rise. A building called Burj Khalifa on the United Arab Emirates city of dubai is 2,722 feets tall. That makes it the tallest building in the world. Until recently, the world's tallest building was in Taipei, Taiwan. this office building, in the heart of the busy capital city, have 101 floors, which is where it gets its name, Taipei 101. Recently, however, engineers and architects in Saudi Arabia began work on a new skyscraper that will surpass both Taipei 101 and Burj Khalifa in height. It 1 kilometer tall. The Kingdom Tower, as it is being called, will be twice as tall as the Burj Khalifa. Adrian Smith, the chief architect says, "the tower will represent the new spirit in Saudi Arabia, which symbolizes the Kingdom as an important global business and cultural leader, and demonstrates the strength and creative vision of its people" With so many tall buildings all over the world, tourists will have to get used to looking up more often.

ON YOUR OWN

Complete one of the following activities.

1. Find a chart or graph that interests you in a newspaper, magazine, or on the Internet and bring it to class. Write a paragraph explaining the information in the chart or graph. Share your chart and paragraph with your classmates.

2. Use the Internet or a library to find unusual facts about an animal from your country. Write a paragraph based on the facts. Use quotes to support some of the information in your paragraph.

LEARNING OUTCOME   **Paragraph Writing:** Write a paragraph describing the steps in a process

When you explain how to do or make something, such as how to program your cell phone or how to make rice and beans, you are explaining a process. Similarly, when you explain how something works or happens, such as how an engine works or how your body digests food, you are also describing a process. When you describe a process, you should organize the steps according to time order.

"Are you ready for me to read the instructions yet?"

PROCESS PARAGRAPHS

Read the model paragraph and underline the topic sentence. Then answer the questions.

Sending Invitations Online

It is easy to send invitations to a party online if you follow these steps. First, choose an online invitation website and click on *create an invitation*. Then, pick an invitation from one of the hundreds they offer. After that, type in the details of your party such as the date, address, and start time. Next, enter all the email addresses of the people you want to invite. Finally, check over the invitation and click *send*. You won't believe how easy it is, and most online invitation sites automatically keep a record of who is coming to your party. I recommend that you try sending online invitations the next time you are giving a party.

1. What steps does the author give?

   a. _____

   b. _____

   c. _____

   d. _____

   e. _____

2. How are the steps organized? _____

Writing Topic Sentences for Process Paragraphs

The topic sentence of a process paragraph must identify the process and often tells something about it. Read the examples.

Examples:

It is not difficult to add a new contact on your smartphone *if you follow these steps.*

You can add a new contact on your smartphone *if you follow these steps.*

It is easy to add a new contact on your smartphone *by following these steps.*

Adding new contacts on your smartphone *is not difficult if you follow these steps.*

Decorating a birthday cake *is fun and easy if you follow these steps.*

PRACTICE **Write a topic sentence for the following paragraphs. Then compare your topic sentences with several of your classmates.**

1.
How to Get a College ID Card

_____ First, get a copy of the receipt that shows you paid your tuition. Then take the receipt to the Student Affairs building. Go to the ID office and show the secretary your receipt. After that, get your picture taken. Remember to smile! Wait three minutes for your picture to be processed and your ID to be printed. Finally, sign your ID card and put it in your wallet.

2.
Addressing an Envelope

_____ First of all, write your name and address in the upper left-hand corner of the envelope. Then write the name and address of the person you are mailing the letter to in the center of the envelope. This usually takes three lines. Put the name on the first line. Write the street address on the second line and the city and state on the third line. Remember to include the zip code. Finally, put a stamp in the upper right-hand corner. The most important thing to remember is to write neatly!

3.

How to Make a Beautiful Flower Arrangement

_____ First, fill a clean vase with water. Second, cut most of the flowers and greens so they are approximately two times the height of your vase. Then, cut a couple of the flowers two inches longer. After you are finished cutting the flowers, you can begin to put the greens in the vase. Now add the other flowers. Start at the outer edge of your vase. Put the longest flowers in the center of your arrangement. Then take a few steps back and admire your bouquet.

4.

Packing a Suitcase

_____ First, collect all the items you want to take and organize everything into groups. For example, put all your shoes in one group, all your clothes in another, all your underwear in a third, and so on. After that, place your shoes on the bottom of the suitcase. Then take your pants, fold them in half, roll them up, and place them in the bottom of the suitcase around the shoes. You can fill empty space on the bottom with socks and underwear. Next, fold and put flat items such as shirts and sweaters as a second layer. Finally, place your last layer of items in the suitcase. This way of packing helps you get organized and stay organized when you travel.

SIGNAL WORDS

WRITER'S TIP: Time Order Signal Words
When you describe a process you put the steps in time order. In order to make the steps clear, you should use time order signal words to guide the reader from one step to the next. Review the time order signal words on page 33.

PRACTICE **Complete the following paragraph using signal words.**

How to Make Popcorn

It is very easy to make good popcorn by following these steps. _____First_____,
put three or four tablespoons of oil in a large heavy pot. _____, heat the oil
on a high flame until one kernel of popcorn pops when you drop it into the hot oil. When
the oil is hot enough, pour one-quarter cup of popcorn into the pot and cover it with a
lid. _____, reduce the flame to medium and begin to shake the pot gently.
Continue shaking the pot until all the corn has popped. _____, empty the
popcorn into a large bowl and add melted butter and salt.

GRAMMAR FOR WRITING: Imperative Sentences

When you explain how to do or make something, you often use *imperative sentences*.
Imperative sentences are different from regular sentences because they do not have a subject.
The implied subject is *you*. Imperative sentences are used to give advice or instructions, or to
express a request or a command.

Study the sentences in the chart. Notice that each one begins with the base form of a verb. For
negative imperative forms use: *Do + not* (*don't*) + base form of the verb.

AFFIRMATIVE SENTENCES	**Fold** the paper in half. **Complete** the application.
NEGATIVE SENTENCES	**Do not take** this medicine during the day. **Don't write** your name on the paper.

PRACTICE **A** Tell someone how to buy a car in your country. Write four affirmative imperative sentences.
Then write four negative imperative sentences.

1. Research the kind of car you want to buy. _____
2. _____
3. _____
4. _____
5. _____
6. _____

7. _____

8. _____

B What would you tell someone about how to give a presentation at work or school? Write four affirmative imperative sentences. Then write four negative imperative sentences.

1. _____

2. _____

3. _____

4. _____

5. _____

6. _____

7. _____

8. _____

ORDERING SENTENCES IN PROCESS PARAGRAPHS

PRACTICE **A** The following sentences describe how to make a chocolate sundae, but they are not in the correct time order. Find the topic sentence and put a *1* in front of it. Use the signal words to help you put the steps in the right order, from *1* to *5*.

How to Make a Sundae

_____ Next, cover the fudge with whipped cream.

_____ Chocolate sundaes are one of the easiest desserts to make.

_____ Finally, sprinkle chopped nuts on the whipped cream and put a cherry on top.

_____ Then pour two tablespoons of hot fudge sauce over the ice cream.

_____ First, put two or three large scoops of your favorite kind of ice cream in a dish.

B Use the steps in exercise A to write a paragraph. Add a title.

_____

_____

_____

_____

_____

_____

_____

_____

_____

_____

C **The following sentences describe what to do if someone is choking. First, find the topic sentence. Then number the sentences in the right order.**

The Heimlich Maneuver

_____ Then make a fist with one hand and grasp the fist with your other hand. Put your hands just below the person's rib cage.

_____ The Heimlich maneuver is a method that anyone can use to help someone who is choking on a piece of food.

_____ Finally, press your fist into the victim's abdomen with a quick upward movement.

_____ The first thing you should do is stand behind the choking person and put your arms around the person's waist.

_____ If the person is still choking, you may need to repeat the maneuver.

D **Now write a paragraph based on the steps in Exercise C. Add a title.**

_____

_____

_____

_____

_____

_____

_____

_____

_____

E Study the pictures. They show how to pot a plant. Use the pictures to number the steps in the correct time order.

_____ Make a hole in the center of soil.

_____ Press the soil down with your thumbs.

__1__ Cover the bottom of the pot with small stones.

_____ Drop the plant into the hole in the soil.

_____ Put two inches of soil on top of the rocks.

_____ Water the plant.

_____ Add soil until it almost reaches the top of the pot.

F Use the steps in Exercise E to complete the paragraph.

How to Pot a Plant

Potting a plant is easy if you follow these steps. _____

_____

_____

_____

_____

_____

_____

_____

_____

_____

WRITING PROCESS PARAGRAPHS

Paragraph Practice 1

Prewriting

A **Choose one of the following processes to write about.**

How to:

- plan a party
- make your favorite dish
- change a flat tire
- get cash from an automatic teller machine
- study for an exam
- program your cell phone
- plant a garden
- send or receive an email

B **Make a list of all the steps in the process and number the steps so they are in the correct time order.**

_____ _____

_____ _____

_____ _____

_____ _____

C **Write a topic sentence that identifies the process and tells something about it.**

_____

Writing

Write the first draft of a paragraph describing the process. Begin with your topic sentence. Use the list of steps from your prewriting as a guide. Include some imperative sentences. Add a title.

_____

_____

_____

_____

_____

_____

_____

_____

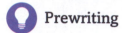

Revising

A Read over your paragraph and look for ways to improve it. Use the Revising Checklist on page 77 to help you. As you revise your paragraph, think about these questions.

1. Are your steps in correct time order?

2. Did you leave out any important steps in the process?

3. Did you use imperative sentences?

B Write your revised paragraph on a separate piece of paper.

Paragraph Practice 2

Prewriting

A Study the diagram. It shows the four stages in the life cycle of a monarch butterfly: eggs, caterpillar, chrysalis, and adult butterfly.

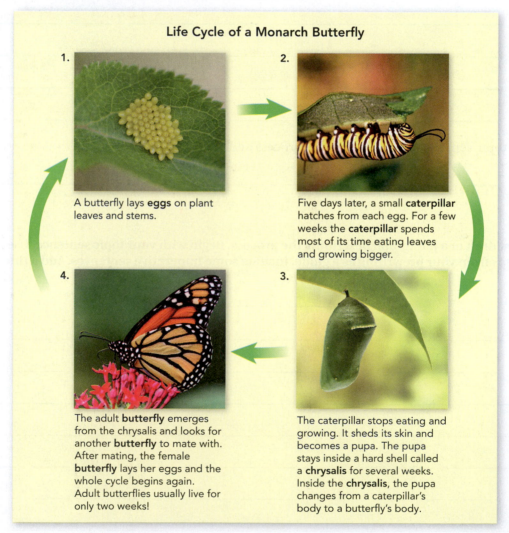

Life Cycle of a Monarch Butterfly

1. A butterfly lays **eggs** on plant leaves and stems.

2. Five days later, a small **caterpillar** hatches from each egg. For a few weeks the **caterpillar** spends most of its time eating leaves and growing bigger.

3. The caterpillar stops eating and growing. It sheds its skin and becomes a pupa. The pupa stays inside a hard shell called a **chrysalis** for several weeks. Inside the **chrysalis**, the pupa changes from a caterpillar's body to a butterfly's body.

4. The adult **butterfly** emerges from the chrysalis and looks for another **butterfly** to mate with. After mating, the female **butterfly** lays her eggs and the whole cycle begins again. Adult butterflies usually live for only two weeks!

B Discuss the four stages in the life cycle with a partner. What happens in each stage? How long does each stage last?

Writing

Use the information from the diagram to write the first draft of a paragraph about the life cycle of a butterfly. Remember to begin with a topic sentence and use signal words. Since you are not giving instructions, but just describing a process, you should not use imperative sentences Add a title.

_____

_____

_____

_____

_____

_____

_____

_____

Revising

A Read over your paragraph and look for ways to improve it. Use the Revising Checklist on page 77 to help you.

B Copy your revised paragraph on a separate piece of paper.

DESCRIBING STEPS IN AN EXPERIMENT

Describing processes is very important in scientific and technical fields.

Study the following lab report.

WATER EXPANSION EXPERIMENT

Purpose: To show that water expands when frozen

Materials: A glass jar, water

Procedure:
1. Fill the glass jar halfway with water.
2. Mark the outside of the jar water level.
3. Put the jar in the freezer until the water freezes.
4. Observe and mark the new water level.

Results: The level of the frozen water is higher.

Read the model paragraph that describes the experiment and answer the questions.

You can do a simple experiment to prove that water expands when it is frozen. All you need is an empty glass jar. First, fill half the jar with water. Then mark the water level on the outside of the jar. After that, put the jar in a freezer until the water freezes. When the water is frozen, take the jar out of the freezer and observe the new water level. You will see that the level of the frozen water is higher. This proves that water expands when it is frozen.

1. What is the topic sentence? _____

_____

2. What signal words are used in the paragraph? _____

_____

3. How many steps are described? _____

Prewriting

Read the following lab report. Discuss it with a classmate.

SOLAR ENERGY EXPERIMENT

Purpose: To show that black is a better collector of solar energy than white

Materials: 2 tin cans, black and white paint, room thermometer

Procedure:
1. Paint the cans—one black, one white.
2. Fill the cans with water.
3. Put the cans in direct sunlight for three hours.
4. Check the temperature of the water in the cans and compare.

Results: The temperature of the water in the black can is higher.

Writing

Now use the lab report to write a paragraph describing the experiment. Remember to begin with a topic sentence and use signal words.

_____

_____

_____

_____

_____

_____

_____

_____

_____

Revising

A Read over your paragraph and look for ways to improve it. Use the Revising Checklist on page 77 to help you.

B Write your revised paragraph on a separate piece of paper.

GIVING DIRECTIONS

When you explain to someone how to get from one place to another, you are giving directions. In order to make your directions clear, you need give step-by-step instructions. It also helps to use words that signal both time order and direction.

Study this list of useful words for writing directions.

DIRECTION SIGNAL WORDS	
Continue	across the street from
Go as far as	between _____ and _____
Go north (or south, east, west)	in the middle of the
Go one block (or two blocks, etc.)	next door to
Go past	on the corner
Go straight (until you come to)	on the left (or the right)
Turn left (or right)	on the left side (or the right side)

A **Look carefully at the map of the historical area of Philadelphia. Find the Visitor Center on the map. Circle it. Tell a partner where it is located.**

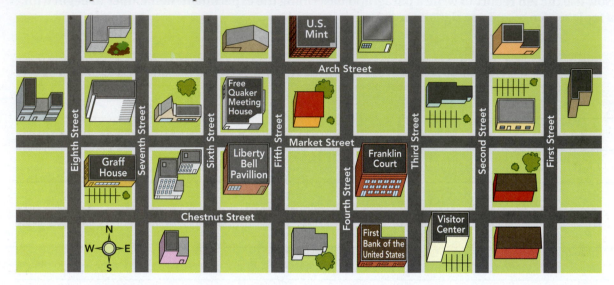

B **Read the directions.**

In order to get from the Visitor Center to the U.S. Mint, follow these directions. First, go north two blocks from the Visitor Center. Then turn left on Arch Street. Continue two blocks on Arch Street to Fifth Street. The U.S. Mint is on your right.

Situation: You work at the Visitor Center. Write directions from the Visitor Center to each of the following places for a tour guidebook.

1. Liberty Bell Pavillion

_____

_____

_____

_____

_____

_____

2. Free Quaker Meeting House

_____

_____

_____

_____

_____

3. First Bank of the United States

_____

_____

_____

_____

_____

4. Franklin Court

_____

_____

_____

_____

_____

5. Graff House

_____

_____

_____

_____

_____

YOU BE THE EDITOR

Read the paragraph. It contains eight mistakes. Correct the mistakes. Copy the corrected paragraph on a separate piece of paper.

How to Remove the Shell From a Lobster

It is not difficult to remove the shell from a lobster if you follow these step. First, to put the lobster on it's back and remove the two large claws and tail section. After that, You must also twist off the flippers at end of the tail section. After these are twisted off, use you fingers to push the lobster meat out of the tail in one piece. Next, removing the black vein. From the tail meat. Finally, before you sit down to enjoy your meal, break open the claws with a nutcracker and remove the meat.

ON YOUR OWN

Choose one of the following activities to complete.

- Draw a simple map of your neighborhood. Label the streets and important buildings. Practice the vocabulary of giving directions by writing directions from your house to several other places. Check your directions by having another student follow them.
- Write a paragraph that tells how to protect yourself when a hurricane, blizzard, tornado, or other natural disaster is forecast for your area.
- Write a paragraph that describes the steps involved in getting a driver's license.

LEARNING OUTCOME

Paragraph Writing: Write a paragraph using descriptive details about a person, place or thing.

Writing a description is like creating a picture using words. The key to writing a good description, is using specific details that create exactly the picture you want. In this chapter you will learn how to write descriptions of people, places, and things.

"This identical twin of yours... Can you describe him?"

DESCRIBING PEOPLE

When you describe a person, you explain what he or she looks and acts like. You write about physical characteristics such as height, weight, and hair color. You can also write about the person's style of clothing and way of talking and walking. The key to writing a good description is to use details that help the reader imagine the person you are describing.

Read the model paragraph, and underline the descriptive details.

An Elegant Thief

The police are searching for a stylish woman who stole a diamond ring from Dayton's Jewelry Store. According to the store manager, the woman has short, curly, brown hair and big blue eyes. She is average height, slender, and about sixty-five years old. When she was last seen, she was elegantly dressed in a grey hat, a black and white plaid coat, black pants, and black, high-heeled boots. She speaks softly and uses her hands a lot when she talks. She doesn't look like someone who would steal a ring!

Lucia: Hi, Clara. I have a big problem and I hope you can help me.

Clara: What's the problem? I'll help if I can.

Lucia: My cousin is coming home tonight from his trip to Europe and I'm supposed to pick him up at the airport at seven o'clock. The problem is that I just found out I have to work late tonight. Can you possibly pick him up for me?

Clara: Sure. What airline is he taking?

Lucia: British Airways. Flight 179.

Clara: OK. But how will I recognize him?

Lucia: Well, he's medium height and average weight.

Clara: That could be almost anyone. Can you be more specific?

Lucia: Well, he has long, curly, blond hair. He wears glasses. I almost forgot! He has a beard.

Clara: What's his name?

Lucia: Ernie Norton.

Clara: OK, no problem. I'll find him.

Lucia: Great. Thank you so much!

Imagine you are Clara. At the last minute, you are unable to go to the airport. Your brother Ben has agreed to pick up Ernie instead. Write a note to Ben describing Ernie so that he will be able to find him. The following questions will help you.

- Is he tall or short?
- Is he fat or thin?
- What color hair does he have?
- Is his hair curly or straight?
- Does he wear glasses?
- Is there anything about him that you notice immediately?

Dear Ben,

_____

_____

_____

_____

_____

_____

_____

Topic Sentences for Descriptive Paragraphs

The topic sentence of a descriptive paragraph should include who or what you are describing and your main impression of the person, place, or thing.

PRACTICE **Read the following sample topic sentences and discuss the questions with a partner.**

1. My grandfather is getting old, but he is still handsome and careful about his appearance.
   a. Who is the writer describing?
   b. How does the author feel about the subject?

2. Although it was made with love, the sweater my aunt gave me is one of the ugliest things I've ever seen.
   a. What is the author describing?
   b. How does the author feel about the object?

3. My most treasured possession is the beautiful pearl ring my grandmother gave me.
   a. What is the author describing?
   b. How does the author feel about the object?

4. My sister's new roommate is absolutely gorgeous.
   a. Who is the author describing?
   b. How does the author feel about her?

5. The first time I met Jason, I thought he appeared frail and sickly.
   a. Who is the author describing?
   b. How does the author feel about him?

6. My favorite piece of furniture is an old, leather armchair that has been in our family room for many years.
   a. What is the author describing?
   b. How does the author feel about the object?

7. Our new teacher is tall and thin and she looks very serious.
   a. Who is the author describing?
   b. How does the author feel about her?

8. I can't wait to get rid of our old, rusty lawn mower.
   a. What is the author describing?
   b. How does the author feel about the object?

WRITING A PARAGRAPH DESCRIBING PEOPLE

When you describe what a person looks like, you write about physical characteristics such as height, weight, and hair color. Here are some words that can help you.

WORDS TO DESCRIBE PEOPLE					
Hair	**Eyes**	**Build**	**Face**	**Age**	**Height**
bald	blue	athletic	beard	in his/her 20s, 30s, 60s	average
black	brown	average	dimple		medium
blond	dark	heavy	freckles	elderly	short
braids	green	medium	heart-shaped	middle-aged	tall
brown	hazel	petite	mole	old	
curly	narrow	plump	mustache	teenage	
dark	oval	slender	oval	young	
long	round	small	round		
ponytail		stocky	square		
red		strong	wrinkles		
shiny		thin			
short					
shoulder-length					
straight					
thick					
thin					
wavy					

Paragraph Practice 1

💡 Prewriting

A Choose someone you know well, such as a friend, relative, teacher, or coworker. Make a list of descriptive details about the person.

_____   _____

_____   _____

_____   _____

B Look over your list. What is your main impression of the person? Use your main impression to write a topic sentence.

_____

✒ Writing

Write the first draft of a description of the person. Add a title.

_____

_____

_____

_____

_____

_____

_____

_____

🔍 Revising

A Read over your description and make sure your descriptive details support your topic sentence. You can also use the Revising Checklist on page 77 to help you.

B Copy your revised description on a separate piece of paper.

Paragraph Practice 2

💡 Prewriting

A Choose someone in your class to describe. Make a list of descriptive details about the person.

_____   _____

_____   _____

_____   _____

B Look over your list. What is your main impression of the person? Use your main impression to write a topic sentence.

_____

✒ Writing

A Write a short description of that person, but do not mention his or her name. Remember to include details about height, hair color, distinguishing features, and so on. Write your description on a separate piece of paper.

B Give the description to your teacher. Your teacher will give you another classmate's description. Read the description you were given. Can you guess who the paragraph describes?

 **Revising**

Did the student reading your paragraph recognize you from the description. If not, revise your paragraph to make it clearer.

JUST FOR FUN

Pretend you are one of the *paparazzi*—photographers who follow famous people and take their pictures. You have just taken a good photo of a famous person and you contact a magazine to try to sell your photo.

A Read the paragraph. What kind of descriptions does the writer include?

> ### Prince William
>
> I have a photograph of Prince William. He is walking on a London street. He is wearing sunglasses and a gray raincoat. He has a new hairstyle. He is carrying a baby girl in a baby sling and walking next to the beautiful Duchess of Cambridge. She is holding hands with a happy-go-lucky little boy. The good-looking couple are both carrying small shopping bags with the name of a famous jeweler on them.

B Find a photo. Write your own description on a separate piece of paper. Name the person. What does he or she look like? What is he or she wearing? What other things or people are in the picture?

DESCRIBING THINGS

Read the model paragraph and answer the questions that follow.

> ### An Antique Watch
>
> I bought a beautiful, antique, gold watch to give my father for his birthday. Although it's more than sixty years old, it's in excellent condition. The round face of the watch is white with shiny raised gold numbers and thin black hands. It's about 36 millimeters in diameter. The back of the watch has a small scratch and the letters *JLH* engraved on it. They are probably the original owner's initials. The band is made of soft brown leather with a gold buckle. I know my father will love the watch because it stills keeps perfect time after all these years.

1. What is the author describing? _____

2. How does the author feel about the object? _____

3. What details does the author use to describe the watch?

   _____   _____

   _____   _____

   _____   _____

4. What is the concluding sentence?

   _____

   _____

Descriptive Details

The supporting sentences in a descriptive paragraph should include details that create a picture with words. They often include information about size, weight, shape, pattern or decoration, color, material, and any special features.

> **WRITER'S TIP:** Sensory Words
>
> When you write a description, you can use words that relate to the senses of sight, sound, touch, smell, and taste. These are called *sensory words*. Sensory words help the reader imagine what you are describing.

Study the list of some common sensory words you can use to describe objects.

COMMON SENSORY WORDS			
Color	**Smell**	**Taste**	**Texture**
black	fresh	bitter	rough
blue	fruity	bland	sharp
orange	mild	fruity	silky
purple	pungent	nutty	smooth
yellow	smoky	oily	soft
	strong	rich	
		salty	
		sour	
		spicy	
		sweet	

Write a few sentences to describe each of the following things. Use sensory words in your descriptions.

1. your favorite food

_____

_____

2. a food you dislike

_____

_____

3. your favorite toy when you were a child

_____

_____

4. your favorite item of clothing

_____

_____

GRAMMAR FOR WRITING: Order of Adjectives

When you use more than one adjective in a series to describe something, they usually follow a certain order. The chart shows the typical order of adjectives in English. However, there are many exceptions and the rules are complicated. Over time, as you learn more English, the order of adjectives will become more natural.

Study the chart and read the example sentences.

Determiner	Opinion	Size	Age	Shape*	Color	Origin	Material	Purpose	Noun
a, an, the	ugly	tiny	old	square	blue	French	cotton	winter	sweater
these	lovely	big	young	round	white	Turkish	metal	sports	hat
four	useful	huge	antique	heavy	yellow	Spanish	gold	shopping	bowl
several	delicious	small	new	long	green	British	plastic	gardening	car
those	pretty	large	ancient	short	orange	Arabic	silk	baseball	watch

* weight and length

Examples:

*I just bought **a soft, Egyptian, cotton towel**.*

*I gave away **an ugly, old, wool sweater**.*

*I can't find **the small, wooden, salad bowl**.*

*She lost her **beautiful, new, gold watch**.*

*We read **two interesting history books** this year.*

PRACTICE **A** Here are some examples from each category of adjectives. Work in a small group. Add two additional adjectives for each item.

1. **Opinion or judgment:** soft, ugly, beautiful, _____ , _____

2. **Size:** small, tall, huge, _____ , _____

3. **Age:** young, old, antique, _____ , _____

4. **Shape:** round, flat, rectangular, _____ , _____

5. **Color:** blue, black, green, _____ , _____

6. **Origin:** Egyptian, Asian, American, _____ , _____

7. **Material:** wooden, metal, glass, _____ , _____

8. **Purpose:** racing (car), baseball (cap), computer (studies), _____ , _____

B Compare your adjectives with another group's.

C Choose the correct order of adjectives to complete the sentence.

1. I invited a(n) _____ student to the meeting.

   a. young engineering intelligent

   b. intelligent young engineering

   c. engineering young intelligent

2. She wore a _____ dress to the party.

   a. lovely blue cotton

   b. cotton blue lovely

   c. blue lovely cotton

3. I found _____ coins in the drawer.

    a. silver three old

    b. old silver three

    c. three old silver

4. The restaurant serves _____ food.

    a. delicious French dinner

    b. French delicious dinner

    c. dinner delicious French

5. There is a(n) _____ table in the corner of the room.

    a. square wooden old

    b. old square wooden

    c. old wooden square

6. I saw a(n) _____ movie last night.

    a. new Japanese exciting

    b. exciting new Japanese

    c. Japanese new exciting

7. The clown wore a _____ hat.

    a. big red plastic

    b. red big plastic

    c. plastic big red

D **Complete the sentences. Write the words in the correct order.**

1. We watched a(n) _____.

    exciting   French   movie   new

2. My roommate is a(n) _____.

    economics   intelligent   Korean   student

3. I bought a(n) _____.

   antique   gold   lovely   ring

4. He gave her a(n) _____.

   expensive   diamond   ring   round

5. I need to borrow a _____.

   gardening   practical   small   tool

6. My sister has _____.

   beautiful   brown   hair   long

7. My best friend is a _____.

   Japanese   musician   talented   young

8. The bride wore a(n) _____.

   dress   elegant   lace   white

WRITER'S TIP: Using Adjectives

Do not use too many adjectives in one sentence. It can confuse your reader. Use only two or three adjectives before a noun.

WRITING A PARAGRAPH DESCRIBING OBJECTS

Paragraph Practice 1

Prewriting

A **Pretend that you have lost something that is special to you. Draw a picture of it and describe the object to a classmate.**

B Make a list of descriptive details about the object. Answer these questions to help you make your list.

- What size is it?
- What shape is it?
- What color is it?

- How heavy is it?
- What are its main characteristics?
- What other thing does it look like?

C Write a topic sentence for your description that includes the object and how you feel about it.

_____

Writing

A Write a description of the object so other people can help you find it. Use the list of descriptive details from your prewriting as a guide.

_____

_____

_____

_____

_____

_____

_____

_____

_____

_____

_____

_____

B Give your description to a classmate and ask him or her to draw the object using only your written description.

Revising

Compare the picture your classmate drew to the description and the picture you drew. How are they alike? What are the differences? The differences should give you clues to help you revise your paragraph. After you revise your paragraph, copy the final draft on a separate piece of paper.

Paragraph Practice 2

Prewriting

A You are going to write a description of something you want to sell online. Before you write a description, read the sample below of a game table for sale on an auction website.

FOR SALE. This beautiful oak game table is a great addition to any room. It is 32 inches in height with four sturdy legs. The top has a 28-inch square game board that can be turned over. One side is for chess or checkers, and the other side is for backgammon. There is also a convenient drawer where you can keep all your game pieces. You will have years of fun with this game table.

B Decide what you want to write a description about. Draw or take a picture of it. Then make a list of descriptive details about the object.

_____   _____

_____   _____

_____   _____

C Write a topic sentence for your description that includes the object and something special about it.

_____

Writing

Write a description of the object you want to sell. Use the list of descriptive details from your prewriting as a guide.

_____

_____

_____

_____

_____

_____

Revising

A Read over your description and make sure the details support your topic sentence. Add any other details to improve your description. Use the Revising Checklist on page 77 to help you.

B Copy your revised description on a separate piece of paper.

PULLING IT ALL TOGETHER

Prewriting

Look around your classroom. Choose something in the room to describe. Think of descriptions you can include of the classroom item.

Writing

Write a short description of the thing you chose, but do not mention what it is. Remember to include details about size, shape, color, texture, and so on.

Revising

A Exchange descriptions with a classmate. Read your classmate's description. Can you guess what it is? Help your classmate revise the description to make it clearer. Use the Revising Checklist on page 77 to help you.

B Copy your revised description on a separate piece of paper.

JUST FOR FUN

You have a small e-commerce business that sells travel goods. This month you are offering a 30-percent-off coupon for new customers on five of your best-selling products. Read the product descriptions for the first two items. Then write descriptions for the other two items.

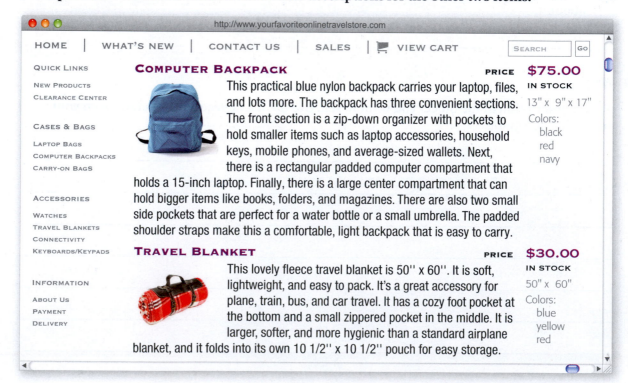

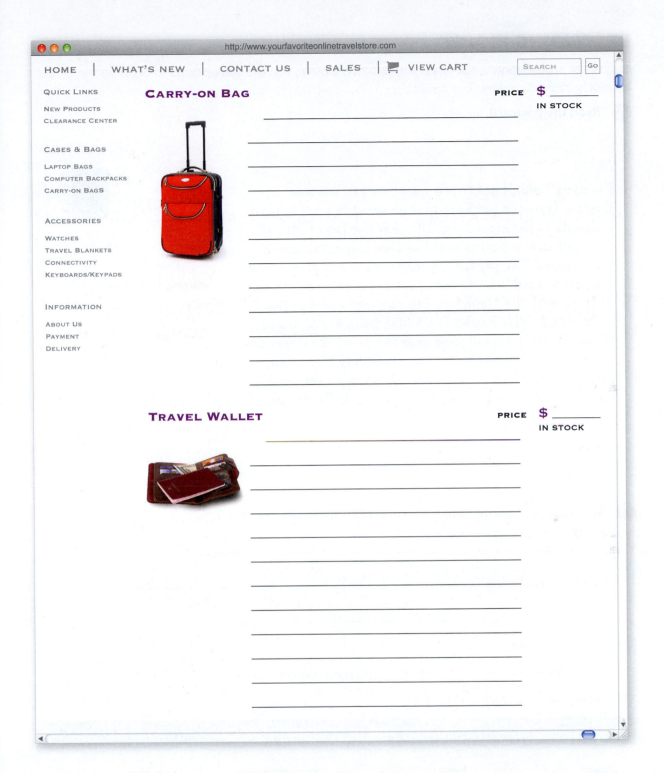

DESCRIBING PLACES

In Chapter 5, you learned that when you describe a place, you use spatial order to organize the details according to their location.

A **Read the postcard.**

Hi,

I'm sorry I didn't get to see you while you were in Boston. It was so hot here that we went to our favorite campsite in the mountains. It's near the top of Mount Greylock in the Berkshires. The view is spectacular in the evening. The sky turns bright orange and pink as the sun sets behind the hills in the distance. From the tower at the top of the mountain, you can look down at the valleys and rivers below. The hiking trails are long and shady. There's a small pond near the campsite where we can swim when we get hot. The site is very clean and rarely crowded. Best of all, there's always a refreshing cool breeze! Let me know when you'll be in Boston again.

Love,

Carolyn

Sharon Laroche
84 Maple Street
Hawthorne, NY 10532

B **What details does Carolyn use to describe Mount Greylock?**

_____   _____

_____   _____

_____   _____

Descriptive Words

Using descriptive language is also important when you describe places.

Study the chart.

WORDS FOR DESCRIBING PLACES			
clean	fresh	mountainous	smoky
cold	hilly	narrow	spectacular
colorful	hot	old	wide
cool	humid	quiet	windy
crowded	industrial	rural	
flat	modern	sandy	

PRACTICE Look at the picture. Pretend you are on vacation there and write a postcard to a friend describing the place. Use at least five descriptive words. Underline the descriptive words you use.

WRITING A PARAGRAPH DESCRIBING PLACES

Paragraph Practice 1

 Prewriting

Talk to your partner about his or her hometown. If you are from the same place, ask your partner questions about another city he or she has visited. Make a list of questions to ask your partner. Use the questions below, or your own questions. Take notes on your partner's answers.

1. What is the name of your hometown and where is it located?

2. How big is it?

3. What are the main geographical features?

4. Are there any interesting stories or historical facts associated with your hometown?

5. What interesting places are to the north, south, east, or west of your hometown?

6. Does your hometown have a college or university?

7. Does your hometown have a shopping mall?

8. What is the most impressive thing about your hometown?

9. What are some interesting things to do and see there?

10. What are the people like?

11. What is the weather like?

 Writing

Use the information you have about your partner's hometown, or a city your partner described, to write the first draft of the paragraph. Be sure to give the name of the place and say something special about it in the topic sentence. Include a title.

_____

_____

_____

_____

_____

_____

_____

Revising

A Ask your partner to read your paragraph. Does he or she have any suggestions? Revise your paragraph based on your partner's suggestions. You can also use the Revising Checklist on page 77 to help you.

B Copy your revised paragraph on a separate piece of paper.

Paragraph Practice 2

Prewriting

A Choose one of the following topics to write about.

- your favorite place to go and relax, such as a beach, a park, or your bedroom
- your favorite place to eat, such as your grandmother's kitchen or a restaurant you like
- your favorite place to go with your friends, such as a mall or a coffee shop

B Make a list of details describing the place.

_____   _____

_____   _____

_____   _____

C Write a topic sentence that names the place and gives your main impression of it.

_____

D Look at your list of details. Cross out details that do not support the topic sentence.

E Choose a pattern of spatial organization, such as left to right or far to near.

Writing

Use your topic sentence and details from your list to write the first draft of the paragraph. Include a title.

_____

_____

_____

_____

_____

_____

_____

Revising

A Read over your description. Use the Revising Checklist on page 77 to help you revise your paragraph. Also, think about these questions as you revise your paragraph.

- Did you include enough specific details about the place?
- What other details can you add to make your description clearer?
- Did you use descriptive words?
- Did you use spatial order to organize the supporting sentences?

B Copy your revised paragraph on a separate piece of paper.

YOU BE THE EDITOR

Read the paragraph. It contains nine mistakes. Correct the mistakes. Copy the corrected paragraph on the lines below.

Dog Missing

My adorable dog, Bette, is missing. She is a black small poodle with browns eyes. She has hair short curly, Bette weighs 8 pounds and is about one and a half feet long. She has a tail short, long floppy ears, and small feet. She is wear a silver collar with an ID tag on it. She is very friendly around people, she loves children. I have had Bette since she was a puppy I miss her very much. I am offering a $50 reward for anyone who finds Bette. Please calling or text me at 555-1212.

_____

_____

_____

_____

_____

_____

_____

ON YOUR OWN

Choose one of the following activities to complete.

- Write a description of one of the people in this picture.

- Write a description of your favorite movie star, musician, or athlete.
- If you could invent something new, what product would you invent? Describe your invention using specific details.
- Describe a well-known building in your hometown.
- Write a description of someone else you know well. It can be a sibling, parent, friend, etc.

....
LEARNING OUTCOME
....

Paragraph Writing: Write a paragraph that expresses your opinion on a number of topics

When you write, it is often necessary to express your opinion. Your goal is to persuade the reader that your opinion is correct. After you state your opinion, you need to give reasons, facts, or examples to support it.

Copyright Randy Glasbergen.
www.glasbergen.com

"The roof leaks, the furnace doesn't work, and the plumbing needs repair . . . but it's located on the greatest planet in the universe"

EXPRESSING OPINIONS

Read the article and the two opinion paragraphs. Answer the questions that follow.

The number of children in public schools in the United States who speak little or no English is increasing rapidly. The overall percentage of students in grades kindergarten through 12 who were born outside of the U.S. is 4.7 percent, or 2.37 million students. But the percent of U.S. students who are considered English language learners is nearly double that: 9.1 percent, or 4.4 million students. In the 2013–14 school year, for example, there were 1.413 million English learners in California public schools. This is 22.7 percent of the total enrollment. Over 2,685,793 students speak a language other than English at home, representing 43.1% of the state's public school enrollment. These students and their teachers face many challenges, including what language to use in the classroom. Some people believe that children who do not speak English should be taught in their native language. Others believe that these children should be taught in English only.

1.

In my opinion, children who do not speak English should be taught in their native language. First of all, these children will feel more comfortable in a strange school if they hear and speak their native language. If they spend most of the day unable to understand what teachers and other students are saying, they may feel lonely and confused. In addition, they will be able to understand subjects like math, history, and science more easily if they are taught in their native language. This way they can concentrate on the new information and not be distracted by understanding a new language at the same time. Finally, there is no research evidence proving that English-only programs are better or even appropriate for children who are still developing their basic linguistic skills. For example, learning how to read for the first time is too complicated in a language that a student does not understand.

a. What is the author's opinion? Underline the sentence that gives his opinion.

b. What three major reasons does the author give to support his opinion?

2.

I believe that children of immigrants should be taught in English. First, they will learn the new language more quickly if all their subjects are taught in English. Students who spend the whole school day listening to English will learn more idioms, general vocabulary, and technical words. Second, children of immigrants will feel less isolated if they are taught in the same language as the rest of the children. They won't be pulled out of some classes and will be able to make friends more easily. Finally, they will be able to perform better on standardized tests if they have learned the material in their classes in English. They will be familiar with standard test instructions in English and will know what kinds of questions to expect.

a. What is the author's opinion? Underline the sentence that gives her opinion.

b. What three major reasons does the author give to support her opinion?

WRITER'S TIP: Using Reasons

A good opinion paragraph should give the reader something to think about. It should include convincing reasons presented in a logical order. It should not include irrelevant reasons that do not support the opinion.

Read the two opinion paragraphs about the Internet. Cross out the irrelevant sentence in each one. Then answer the questions.

1.

Getting Information on the Internet

In my opinion, the Internet is the most valuable tool we have today for getting information. No matter what or who you're looking for, you can probably find the information you need quickly and easily on the Internet. Information that used to be difficult or time-consuming to find is now just a few clicks away. For example, by using search engines on the Internet, it's easy to locate long lost friends or family members. You can find prices and other information on products you want to buy, too. In addition, you can find scholarly information on almost any topic you want to study even if you don't have access to a university library. From literature and history, to medicine and music, the Internet has thousands of Web sites dedicated to providing information. This means that everyone has equal access to information. The word *Internet* was first used in 1982. Finally, the Internet allows new information to be transmitted almost instantly. As soon as something happens in the news, you can read about it on the Internet. In today's world, where the more you know the better off you are, the Internet may very well hold the key to success!

a. What is the author's opinion? Underline the sentence that gives her opinion.

b. What three major reasons does the author give to support her opinion?

_____

_____

_____

2.

Too Much Information on the Internet

I think there is too much information available on the Internet today. First of all, much of the information on the Internet is unreliable and misleading. With no one regulating or fact-checking what is put on the Internet, it is very hard to know if the information you're reading is even true. It's easy to find the definition of a word on the Internet. In addition, much of the information that is readily available on the Internet can be dangerous in the wrong hands. For instance, it is easy to gain access to other people's personal information. Pictures, names, addresses, and phone numbers are only a few clicks away. Even credit card numbers are easy for hackers * to access. Finally, all of this information can lead to something called "information overload." If you don't know what information overload is, don't worry. There is a lot of information about it on the Internet! Basically, information overload happens when you have too much information to make a decision or remain informed about a topic. In conclusion, there is definitely far too much information on the Internet—some of which is personal, dangerous, or simply false.

* A hacker is someone who secretly, and without permission, uses or changes the information in other people's computer systems.

a. What is the author's opinion? Underline the sentence that gives his opinion.

b. What three major reasons does the author give to support his opinion?

_____

_____

_____

Topic Sentences That Express an Opinion

When your topic sentence is an opinion, you can begin the sentence with one of these phrases.

- I am against
- I am in favor of
- I believe (that)
- I oppose

- I support
- I think (that)
- In my opinion,

PRACTICE **Write a topic sentence for each paragraph.**

1.

The Benefits of Public Transportation

_____ First of all, more public transportation helps solve the traffic problem in our city. Secondly, public transportation provides an inexpensive means of transportation for people who cannot afford to buy cars. Most importantly, public transportation is better for the environment because it produces less air pollution.

2.

Working Part-time

_____ The most obvious point is that you can earn extra money. Secondly, working part-time and going to school will help you learn to manage your time more effectively. Hopefully, this will make you a more organized person. Finally, you can gain some work experience that will help you get a better job when you graduate.

3.

The Importance of Genetically Modified Plants

_____ First of all, genetically modified (GM) plants can survive weed killers. That means they require less chemical spraying. Many GM plants even produce their own insecticides. Planting GM crops also lowers farmers' costs. Finally, when farmers plant GM crops, they increase their output. That means more food at a lower cost.

OUTLINING AN OPINION PARAGRAPH

You practiced making a simple outline in Chapter 6. Now you will make a more detailed outline. An outline is a good way to organize your ideas. Organize the ideas in the order you plan to use them when you write.

Prewriting

A **Discuss the sentences with a partner. Decide which ones support the opinion that watching TV is good for children. Mark those with a _G_. Also decide which sentences support the opinion that watching TV is bad for children. Mark those with a _B_.**

_B_ 1. Watching TV is too passive.

_____ 2. Watching TV can be an educational experience.

_____ 3. There is too much violence on TV.

_____ 4. TV provides windows to different countries, cultures, and languages.

_____ 5. Children get a biased picture of society from TV.

_____ 6. TV gives children free entertainment and a time to relax quietly.

_____ 7. Children are too influenced by the commercials they see on TV.

B Fill in the outlines. The topic sentences are given. Use the sentences from Exercise A as main supporting points. You will fill in the details later.

1. **Topic sentence:** In my opinion, watching TV is good for children.

   Main supporting point 1: _Watching TV can be an educational experience._

   Detail: _Many TV shows teach children about science, history, and the arts._

   Detail: _Educational shows can help develop children's socialization and_

   learning skills.

   Main supporting point 2: _____

   Detail: _____

   _____

   Detail: _____

   _____

   Main supporting point 3: _____

   Detail: _____

   _____

   Detail: _____

   _____

2. **Topic sentence:** I believe that watching TV is bad for children.

   Main supporting point 1: _____

   Detail: _____

   _____

   Detail: _____

   _____

   Main supporting point 2: _____

   Detail: _____

   _____

   Detail: _____

Main supporting point 3: _____

Detail: _____

_____

Detail: _____

_____

Main supporting point 4: _____

Detail: _____

_____

Detail: _____

_____

C **Now read and discuss the list of sentences that follow. They are details that go with the main supporting points in the outline. Complete the outlines in Exercise B by writing each detail under the appropriate major supporting points.**

- TV provides a pleasant escape from the stress that many children experience.
- TV shows often reinforce negative gender and racial stereotypes.
- Many TV shows teach children about science, history, and the arts.
- Documentaries show children what is going on in different parts of the world.
- Children in the United States see 40,000 commercials each year.
- There are more than seven acts of violence per hour on prime-time TV.
- Instead of watching TV, children should be doing creative activities and spending more time outdoors.
- Cartoons are often violent with the violence portrayed as funny, disguising the real effects of violence.
- Educational shows can help develop children's socialization and learning skills.
- Children can't distinguish program content from commercials, especially when TV characters promote the products.
- Some TV shows teach children both English and Spanish.
- Studies show that children who watch too much television are more likely to be overweight.
- Children often think that problems can be resolved in a half hour, like they often are on TV.
- Some studies show that children experience a soothing effect by watching cartoons.

Writing from an Outline

The principal of an elementary school asked you to write a short article that expresses your opinion about children and TV for the school newsletter. What is your opinion? Use your opinion as the topic sentence. Use one of the outlines to help you write the paragraph. Include a title.

_____

_____

_____

_____

_____

_____

_____

_____

_____

_____

Revising

A Read your article and look for ways to improve it. Use the Revising Checklist on page 77 to help you.

B Copy your revised paragraph on a separate piece of paper. Put it in your writing folder.

> ### GRAMMAR FOR WRITING: Run-On Sentences
>
> You have learned how to correct comma splices and sentence fragments. Now you will learn how to correct another common problem, **run-on sentences**. A run-on sentence occurs when you write two complete sentences as one sentence without punctuation.
>
> **Examples:**
>
> INCORRECT: *Sue loves to cook she is always in the kitchen.* (run-on sentence)
>
> CORRECT: *Sue loves to cook. She is always in the kitchen.*
>
> INCORRECT: *I haven't eaten all day I'm very hungry.* (run-on sentence)
>
> CORRECT: *I haven't eaten all day. I'm very hungry.*

There are several ways to correct run-on sentences. Study three common ways in the chart.

Solution	Example
Divide the run-on into two separate sentences. Use a period after each sentence. Begin the second sentence with a capital letter.	**Run-on sentence:** Pat loves to swim he is often in the pool. **Correct sentence:** Pat loves to swim. He is often in the pool.
Use a **coordinating conjunction** (*and, but, so*) to make a compound sentence. Use a comma before the conjunction.	**Run-on sentence:** The movie was boring we watched it anyway. **Correct sentence:** The movie was boring, but we watched it anyway.
Divide the run-on sentence into two clauses. Then, join the two clauses with a *semi-colon* (;). NOTE: Be careful not to overuse the semi-colon. The semi-colon is usually used between two main clauses that are closely related in meaning and grammatical form.	**Run-on sentence:** Mi-sook wants to pass her driving test she practices driving with her father every day. **Correct sentence:** Mi-sook wants to pass her driving test; she practices driving with her father every day.

PRACTICE **A Correct the run-on sentences by making two separate sentences.**

1. It is supposed to rain this afternoon we postponed our picnic.

   _____

2. Jane is always late for class the other students and teacher think her behavior is rude.

   _____

3. It's after midnight I'm getting sleepy.

   _____

4. The project was difficult we worked hard to finish it on time.

   _____

5. The roads are slippery you should drive carefully.

   _____

B Correct the run-on sentences using coordinating conjunctions.

1. We followed the directions we ended up at the wrong place.

   _____

2. I got a good grade on my exam I am very happy.

   _____

3. You can call me you can send me a text.

_____

4. Most people liked the movie I thought it was boring.

_____

5. My computer is broken I borrowed my roommate's.

_____

C **Correct the run-on sentences using semi-colons.**

1. The cake has been baking for an hour you should take it out of the oven.

_____

2. Henry is cold and wet he wants to go inside.

_____

3. Alicia likes to read she belongs to two book clubs.

_____

4. I'm not very good at chess I usually lose when I play.

_____

5. Frank likes to exercise he goes to the gym every day.

_____

D **Write _C_ in front of the complete sentences. Write _R_ in front of the run-on sentences. Then correct the run-on sentences using one of the ways in the chart.**

<u>R</u> **1.** I like my teacher she is very helpful.

<u>I like my teacher. She is very helpful.</u>

_____ **2.** This book is very confusing I can't understand it.

_____

_____ **3.** It was too hot to play tennis we decided to postpone the game.

_____

_____ **4.** Steve makes a lot of money, but he works too hard.

_____

_____ 5. I enjoy going to restaurants my husband prefers to eat at home.

_____

_____ 6. Some people go to college full-time others go part-time.

_____

_____ 7. I got an A on my English test I was very happy.

_____

_____ 8. It is a beautiful summer day; there isn't a cloud in the sky.

_____

_____ 9. Hala has a toothache she needs to go to the dentist.

_____

_____ 10. I'd like to move to California the weather is usually nice there.

_____

E Compare your sentences with a partner.

WRITING OPINION PARAGRAPHS

Paragraph Practice 1

 Prewriting

A Discuss the following topics in small groups. Talk about the pros and cons of each situation. Fill in the chart with your group's ideas. Then write a sentence that expresses your own personal opinion on each topic.

1. Mothers with small children working outside the house

PROS	CONS

Opinion statement: In my opinion, _____

_____

2. Using nuclear power to solve the energy crisis

PROS	CONS

Opinion statement: _____

_____

3 Using animals in laboratory experiments

PROS	CONS

Opinion statement: _____

_____

4. Using the death penalty as a form of criminal punishment

PROS	CONS

Opinion statement: _____

_____

5. Cloning plants and animals

PROS	CONS

Opinion statement: _____

_____

6. Using the Internet to do research

PROS	CONS

Opinion statement: _____

_____

B Choose one of your opinion statements from Exercise A . Look at the your group's ideas and add any other ideas that you think are important. Cross out ideas that you don't want to use.

C Complete the outline. Choose three reasons for your main supporting points. Add details to strengthen each one. List your reasons in order of importance.

Opinion statement: _____

Reason 1: _____

Detail(s): _____

_____

Reason 2: _____

Detail(s): _____

_____

Reason 3: _____

Detail(s): _____

_____

✎ Writing

Write the first draft of an opinion paragraph. Use your opinion statement as the topic sentence. Then use your reasons and details to support your opinion. Use some of the words that signal order of importance that you learned in Chapter 4. Remember, your purpose is to convince readers that your opinion is correct. Include a title.

_____

_____

_____

_____

_____

_____

_____

_____

_____

_____

🔍 Revising

Ⓐ **Read your paragraph and look for ways to improve it. As you revise your paragraph, think about these questions.**

- Does the topic sentence state your opinion?
- Do you have three reasons to support your opinion?
- Do you have some details to make your paragraph more complete?
- Have you used signal words to introduce your reasons?
- Are there any irrelevant sentences your need to cross out?
- Do you have any run-on sentences you need to correct?

Ⓑ **Copy your revised paragraph on a separate piece of paper.**

Paragraph Practice 2

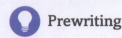 **Prewriting**

A Read the letter to the editor a woman sent to her local newspaper. Then discuss the letter in small groups.

Dear Editor:

Last month our nine-year-old daughter was hit by a car. The man driving the car was talking on his cell phone at the time and didn't stop at a stop sign. Our little girl was in the hospital for three long weeks. My husband and I didn't know if she would be able to walk again. It was a terrible time for us. Although today she is alive and well, we are afraid something like that might happen again.

Recently, we heard that the punishment for the driver was only a $500 fine. He didn't go to jail, and he didn't lose his license. Today, he is free to drive and possibly commit the same crime again. Maybe next time he will kill somebody.

We feel the laws against talking on a cell phone and driving should be very strict. These drivers should pay for their crimes. We think their licenses should be taken away. We need stricter laws!

Kathleen Johnson
Philadelphia, PA

B Discuss these questions with the people in your group.

1. Do you think driving while talking on a cell phone is a serious crime?

2. Which of the following do you think is a fair punishment for people convicted of driving and talking on a cell phone? Why?
   - lose their license
   - be sent to jail
   - lose their car
   - pay a fine of $500 or more
   - get a traffic ticket
   - other: _____

3. What is the punishment in the country where you live now?

Writing

Write the first draft of an opinion paragraph about talking on a cell phone and driving.

_____

_____

_____

_____

_____

Revising

A   **Revise your paragraph. Use the Revising Checklist on page 77 to help you.**

B   **Add one or more of these facts to your paragraph. Put it in your writing folder.**

- Research shows that talking on a cell phone slowed drivers' reactions to seeing a pedestrian enter a crosswalk by 40 percent.

- 14 states, D.C., Puerto Rico, Guam and the U.S. Virgin Islands prohibit all drivers from using hand-held cell phones while driving.

- A major American insurance company reports that distracted driving due to cell phone use causes millions of injuries and deaths, and billions of dollars in damages annually.

Paragraph Practice 3

Prewriting

Read and discuss the news article and the police report. Who do you think committed the crime?

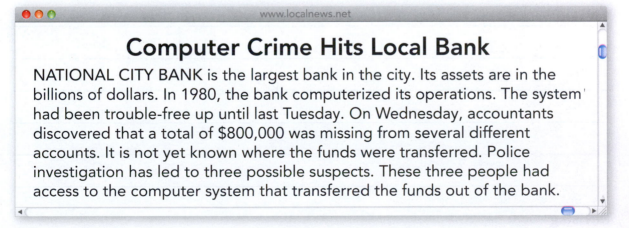

www.localnews.net

Computer Crime Hits Local Bank

NATIONAL CITY BANK is the largest bank in the city. Its assets are in the billions of dollars. In 1980, the bank computerized its operations. The system had been trouble-free up until last Tuesday. On Wednesday, accountants discovered that a total of $800,000 was missing from several different accounts. It is not yet known where the funds were transferred. Police investigation has led to three possible suspects. These three people had access to the computer system that transferred the funds out of the bank.

POLICE REPORT

POSSIBLE SUSPECTS

(a) Norman Glass—computer operator
- has worked at bank for 6 months
- earns low salary
- has wife and four children
- lives in large house and drives expensive new car
- before working at bank he served five years in army (won a Medal of Honor)

(b) Richard Allen—vice president of bank
- has worked at bank for 35 years
- has a good history with bank
- recently lost a lot of money in stock market
- takes expensive vacations
- earns very high salary

(c) Jim Tomlin—branch manager
- has worked at bank for 2 years
- is active in church and community
- graduated top of his class at Harvard
- supports sick mother who lives in an expensive nursing home
- has a gambling problem

 Writing

Write a paragraph stating your opinion about who committed the crime. Be sure to give specific reasons to support your opinion. Add a title.

_____

_____

_____

_____

_____

_____

_____

_____

 Revising

A Read your paragraph and look for ways to improve it. Use the Revising Checklist on page 77 to help you.

B Copy your revised paragraph on a separate piece of paper.

Paragraph Practice 4

Prewriting

A Your school is hiring a new English instructor. You have been asked to join a committee that will help select the instructor. In a group, read and discuss these two résumés from possible candidates.

Lynn Whitnall
Plaza de la Paz, No.2
CP 36000 Guanajuato
Gto, Mexico
+52 (473) 732-02-13
l.whitnall@email.com

POSITION DESIRED:
English instructor

EDUCATION
1995 BA Spanish, New York University

EMPLOYMENT

2008–present	Spanish teacher, International High School
2006–2008	English Instructor, Tokyo Girls High School
2004–2006	Peace Corps volunteer in Colombia

OTHER
Fluent in Spanish, Arabic, Japanese

AWARDS
Excellence in Teaching Award, 2013

Debra Fines
42 St. James Place
Philadelphia, PA 19106
(215) 555-9008
debraf@bestmail.net

Position Desired:
English Instructor

Education:

1993–97	BA English, McGill University
1998	MA English, University of Toronto
2000	PhD Linguistics, University of Pennsylvania

Employment Experience

2005–present	Consultant and Author
2000–2005	Instructor, Intensive English Program, University of Vermont
1999–2000	Teaching Assistant, Linguistics Department, University of Pennsylvania
1998–1999	Swimming Teacher
1993–1998	Server, Chez Robert

Publication:
English Verb Tenses, Shortman Publishing Company, 2006

Personal:
Fluent in French; competitive swimmer

Writing

Who would you hire for the job? Write a paragraph supporting your decision. Include a title.

_____

_____

_____

_____

_____

_____

_____

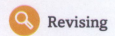
Revising

A Read your paragraph and look for ways to improve it. Use the Revising Checklist on page 77 to help you.

B Copy your revised paragraph on a separate piece of paper.

YOU BE THE EDITOR

Read the paragraph. It contains eleven mistakes. Correct the mistakes. Copy the corrected paragraph on a separate piece of paper.

Suleiman the Magnificent

In me opinion, Suleiman was one of the greatest leaders of all time he accomplished more than any other ruler of the Ottoman Empire. During his reign at 1520 to 1566, Suleiman expanding the size of the Ottoman Empire to include parts of Asia, europe, and Africa. While Suleiman's military victories made him a well-respected world leader. He did many other important things for the empire as well. For example Suleiman introduced a new system of law. he also promoted education, architecture, and the arts. Therefore, I belief he deserves the name "Suleiman the Magnificent."

ON YOUR OWN

Write a paragraph giving your opinion on one of the following topics.
- following a vegetarian diet
- businesses that only care about making a profit
- enjoying your money when you earn it rather than saving it for the future
- access to good healthcare is a right, not a privilege
- shopping online
- taking college courses online

Paragraph Writing: Write a paragraph comparing or contrasting two people, experiences, or things

Very often in your writing you will need to explain how things are similar or different. When you *compare* two things, you explain how they are similar. When you *contrast* two things, you explain how they are different.

" BUT, DAD, ALL SNOWMEN ARE DIFFERENT, 'CAUSE ALL SNOWFLAKES ARE DIFFERENT. "

COMPARING

Read the model paragraph. Underline the topic sentence. Answer the question.

Mistaking Identical Twins

Ann and Beth are alike in many ways. They are identical twins, so it's easy to understand the embarrassing mistake I made yesterday. I was planning to invite Ann to my parent's house for Thanksgiving dinner, but it turned out I asked Beth. The two sisters look exactly alike. Ann is tall and thin with short, curly, brown hair. Likewise, Beth is a tall, thin girl with short, curly, brown hair. They also have the same unusual blue-green eye color. In addition, Ann wears gold-rimmed glasses and so does Beth. Finally, both Ann and Beth have freckles. I wouldn't be surprised if they even have the exact same number of freckles. Now I have to explain my mistake to both of them. I'll just tell my parents both girls are coming!

What similarities about Ann and Beth does the author write about?

_____ _____

_____ _____

_____ _____

Signal Words of Comparison

English has many words and sentence patterns to show comparisons.

Study the chart.

Signal Words of Comparison	Examples
*_similarly_	Tokyo has an efficient subway system. **Similarly**, London has an efficient subway system.
*_likewise_	Tokyo has an efficient subway system. **Likewise**, London has an efficient subway system.
both … _and_	**Both** London **and** Tokyo have efficient subway systems.
_as_ + adjective + _as_	Tokyo's subway system is **as** efficient **as** London's.
the same + noun + _as_	My car is **the same** color **as** yours.
be alike/_be similar_ (_in several ways_, _in three ways_, _in many ways_) _be alike_ and _be similar_ have the same meaning	Squash and racquetball **are alike** in several ways. Squash and racquetball **are similar** in several ways.
be similar to/_be like_ + a noun _be similar to_ and _be like_ have the same meaning	The weather in Philadelphia **is similar to** the weather in Istanbul. The weather in Philadelphia **is like** the weather in Istanbul.

*_Similarly_ and _likewise_ are used at the beginning of a sentence to signal to the reader that an idea expressed in that sentence is similar to an idea expressed in the previous sentence. Remember to use a comma after _similarly_ or _likewise_.

PRACTICE **A** **Read the pairs of sentences. Write three sentences of comparison for each pair. Use the words given.**

Soccer teams have eleven players. American football teams have eleven players.

a. (likewise) <u>_Soccer teams have eleven players. Likewise, American football teams have eleven players._</u>

b. (both . . . and) *Both soccer teams and American football teams have eleven players.*

c. (the same . . . as) *Soccer teams have the same number of players as American football teams.*

1. Bats hibernate in winter. Bears hibernate in winter.

   a. (similarly) _____

   b. (likewise) _____

   c. (both . . . and) _____

2. Learning to write well takes a lot of practice. Learning to drive a car takes a lot of practice.

   a. (both . . . and) _____

   b. (likewise) _____

   c. (similarly) _____

3. Sunlight is a source of renewable energy. Wind is a source of renewable energy.

   a. (similarly) _____

   b. (both . . . and) _____

   c. (likewise) _____

4. The winter in Moscow is long and cold. The winter in Anchorage is long and cold.

   a. (alike) _____

   b. (likewise) _____

   c. (like) _____

5. My car is new and reliable. Your car is new and reliable.

   a. (similarly) _____

   b. (both . . . and) _____

   c. (be alike) _____

6. My hometown is small and historic. Your hometown is small and historic.

   a. (similar to) _____

   b. (both . . . and) _____

   c. (be alike in) _____

B Practice writing comparisons with the nouns and adjectives given. Use *as* + adjective + *as* for adjectives. Use *the same* + noun + *as* for nouns.

1. Danny weighs 185 pounds. Arthur weighs 185 pounds.

   (noun: *weight*) *Danny is the same weight as Arthur.* _____

   (adjective: *heavy*) *Danny is as heavy as Arthur.* _____

2. Mary is five feet tall. John is five feet tall.

   (noun: *height*) _____

   (adjective: *tall*) _____

3. This new car costs $18,500. That used car costs $18,500.

   (noun: *price*) _____

   (adjective: *expensive*) _____

4. My house has twelve rooms. Your house has twelve rooms.

   (noun: *size*)_____

   (adjective: *big*) _____

5. Jackson was born in 1982. Paul was born in 1982.

   (noun: *age*) _____

   (adjective: *old*) _____

6. This short story is seventy pages long. That story is seventy pages long.

   (noun: *length*) _____

   (adjective: *long*) _____

GRAMMAR FOR WRITING: Sentence Patterns of Comparison

Study these comparisons using *and* with *so*, *too*, *either*, and *neither*. Notice that they are ways to compare sentences and clauses that have similar information. Using these patterns will make your writing more natural. They are like a shortcut for writing out a complete clause.

Study the charts.

Explanation	Examples
We use *so* or *too* with two affirmative sentences that express similar ideas. Use *and* to connect the similar ideas. Put a comma before *and*. Notice that the second verb agrees with the second subject (singular or plural).	**Sentences with the verb *be*:** Cathy is a medical student, and Ashley is a medical student. → Cathy is a medical student **and** Ashley **is, too**. *Cathy is a medical student, **and so is** Ashley. Amy and Rose are twins, and Stan and Fred are twins. → Amy and Rose are twins, **and** Stan and Fred **are, too**. Amy and Rose are twins, **and so are** Stan and Fred. We are excited about the trip, and Susan is excited about the trip. → We are excited about the trip, **and** Susan **is, too**. We are excited about the trip **and so is** Susan. **Sentences with other verbs:** Japan exports cars, and Korea exports cars. → Japan exports cars, **and** Korea **does, too**. *Japan exports cars, **and so does** Korea. The libraries open at 9:00 and the computer labs open at 9:00. → The libraries open at 9:00, **and** the computer labs **do, too**. *The libraries open at 9:00, **and so do** the computer labs. The libraries open at 9:00 and the cafeteria opens at 9:00. → The libraries open at 9:00 **and** the cafeteria **does, too**. *The libraries open at 9:00, **and so does** the cafeteria.
We use *neither* or *not either* (*isn't/aren't either*) with negative sentences that express similar ideas. Notice that the second verb agrees with the second subject (singular or plural).	**Sentences with *be*:** The blue dress isn't expensive, **and** the green dress **isn't either**. *The blue dress isn't expensive, **and neither is** the green dress. This book isn't interesting, **and neither are** these magazines. These magazines aren't interesting, and **neither is** this book. The blue dresses aren't expensive, **and** the green dresses **aren't either**. The blue dresses aren't expensive, **and neither are** the green dresses. **Sentences with other verbs:** Owls don't sleep at night, **and** mice **don't either**. *Owls don't sleep at night, **and neither do** mice. **Jason doesn't** get up early, and **his son doesn't either**. *Jason doesn't** get up early, and **neither does his son**. **Olivia doesn't** go to bed late, **and** her roommates **don't either**. **Olivia doesn't** go to bed late, **and neither do** her roommates.

* Notice the word order in sentences with *so* and *neither*. The subject comes after the verb.

Combine each set of the affirmative sentences in two ways. Follow the example.

1. Judy runs four miles a day, and her roommate runs four miles a day.

   a. <u>*Judy runs four miles a day, and her roommate does, too.*</u>

   b. <u>*Judy runs four miles a day, and so does her roommate.*</u>

2. Mark plays the piano, and Dave plays the piano.

   a. _____

   b. _____

3. The bank opens at 9:30 A.M., and the grocery store opens at 9:30 A.M.

   a. _____

   b. _____

4. Jamaica is sunny and beautiful, and Hawaii and Miami are sunny and beautiful.

   a. _____

   b. _____

5. Skiing and snowboarding are exciting sports, and surfing is an exciting sport.

   a. _____

   b. _____

6. Philadelphia is an old city, and Boston is an old city.

   a. _____

   b. _____

7. Suzanne lives in a small apartment, and Dave and his brother live in a small apartment.

   a. _____

   b. _____

B **Combine each of the negative sentences in two ways. Follow the example.**

1. Peter doesn't smoke and Alex doesn't smoke.

   a. *Peter doesn't smoke, and neither does Alex.*

   b. *Peter doesn't smoke, and Alex doesn't either.*

2. The Browns don't have a car, and the Johnsons don't have a car.

   a. _____

   b. _____

3. Suzi doesn't live in the dorm, and Don doesn't live in the dorm.

   a. _____

   b. _____

4. Charlie isn't friendly, and Liz and her roommate aren't friendly.

   a. _____

   b. _____

5. Maria doesn't have a driver's license, and Orhan doesn't have a driver's license.

   a. _____

   b. _____

6. My calculus course isn't easy, and my physics course isn't easy.

   a. _____

   b. _____

7. I don't work on the weekends, and my wife doesn't work on the weekends.

   a. _____

   b. _____

Writing Topic Sentences for Comparison Paragraphs

When you write the topic sentence for a comparison paragraph, you must state the two things that you are comparing. Look at the following topic sentences.

- *Time Out and The Blue Gills are very similar bands.*
- *My two favorite bands, Time Out and The Blue Gills, have several things in common.*
- *The rock bands Time Out and The Blue Gills are alike in many ways.*
- *Time Out and The Blue Gills share many similarities.*
- *Time Out is similar to The Blue Gills in several ways.*

PRACTICE **Write a topic sentence for each of the following paragraphs.**

1.

Two Cities, Similar Weather

_____ First of all, both cities are hot and humid most of the year. The typical daytime temperature in both places is about 92 degrees Fahrenheit (33 degrees Celsius) with humidity of 99 percent. It also rains a lot during the summer in Hill View. Likewise, it rains almost every day in Valley Ridge in the summer. Finally, the evenings and nights are warm in Hill View, and so are the evenings in Valley Ridge.

2.

Similar Dogs

_____ The main similarity is that both dogs are very friendly. Spot loves people, and so does Freckles. In addition, both of my dogs are smart and can do lots of tricks. For example, both can roll over on command. Another similarity is that both dogs are picky eaters. They only like the most expensive canned dog food. Spot doesn't like dry dog food, and neither does Freckles.

3.

Similar Magazines

_____ First of all, they have many of the same sections. For example, *The Reporter* and *The Monitor* both have sections on politics, finance, science, and culture. In addition, both of these popular magazines cost $12.99, and both are read by millions of people around the world. They also have the same cover story almost every week, and they usually review the same books and movies in their culture sections. Another similarity between the two magazines is their point of view. *The Reporter* is very conservative, and so is *The Monitor*. Finally, both magazines are available online.

WRITING PARAGRAPHS OF COMPARISON

Paragraph Practice 1

Prewriting

Write four sentences comparing Stephanie Brooks and Ann Friedman. Base your comparisons on the information provided on their student ID cards.

Compton Community College

Stephanie Brooks
Major: Nursing
Date of birth: 7/16/1996
Valid through 06/2020

Compton Community College

Ann Friedman
Major: Nursing
Date of birth: 7/16/1996
Valid through 06/2020

1. _____

2. _____

3. _____

4. _____

Writing

Use your sentences to write the first draft of a paragraph comparing Stephanie and Ann. Remember to begin with a topic sentence and use some sentence patterns and signal words that show comparison. Include a title.

_____

_____

_____

_____

_____

_____

_____

_____

_____

A Read your paragraph and look for ways to improve it. Use the Revising Checklist on page 77 to help you.

B Copy your revised paragraph on a separate piece of paper.

Paragraph Practice 2

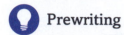 Prewriting

Read the following ads. Write four sentences of comparison based on your observations and the information provided.

1. _____

2. _____

3. _____

4. _____

 Writing

Use your sentences to write the first draft of a paragraph comparing the two hoodies.

_____

_____

_____

_____

_____

_____

Revising

A Read your paragraph and look for ways to improve it. Use the Revising Checklist on page 77 to help you.

B Copy your revised paragraph on a separate piece of paper.

Paragraph Practice 3

Prewriting

A Study this biographical information about two important Americans, John Adams and Thomas Jefferson.

John Adams

Born: October 19, 1735

Died: July 4, 1826

- important person in the American Revolution
- delegate to the Continental Congress
- signer of Declaration of Independence
- studied and practiced law
- second U.S. president
- father of the sixth U.S. president—John Quincy Adams

Thomas Jefferson

Born: April 13, 1743

Died: July 4, 1826

- played important role in American Revolution
- delegate to the Continental Congress
- author and signer of Declaration of Independence
- third president of United States
- foreign minister to France
- founded University of Virginia
- studied and practiced law
- philosopher, architect, inventor

B Make a list of the similarities between the two men.

_____   _____

_____   _____

_____   _____

C Write a topic sentence for your paragraph.

_____

✏️ Writing

Write the first draft of a paragraph comparing Adams and Jefferson. Use your list of similarities as a guide. Include a title.

_____

_____

_____

_____

_____

_____

_____

_____

🔍 Revising

A Read your paragraph and look for ways to improve it. Use the Revising Checklist on page 77 to help you.

B Copy your revised paragraph on a separate piece of paper.

Paragraph Practice 4

💡 Prewriting

A Choose one of the following topics to compare. Brainstorm a list of similarities between the two things you are comparing.

- two movies you have seen
- two professional athletes you admire
- two restaurants you have been to

- two teachers you have had
- two sports you enjoy
- two people you know

_____   _____

_____   _____

_____   _____

B Write a topic sentence for your paragraph. Be sure to identify the two things you are comparing.

_____

Writing

Write the first draft of a paragraph of comparison. Use your list of similarities as a guide. Use *similarly* or *likewise* in at least one sentence. Include a title.

_____

_____

_____

_____

_____

_____

_____

_____

_____

Revising

A Look for ways to improve your paragraph. Think about these questions.

1. Are there any other similarities you should include?

2. Can you add a concluding sentence?

3. Did you use signal words correctly?

4. Did you use *similarly* and *likewise* correctly?

5. Did you use different sentence patterns to make your comparisons?

B Copy your revised paragraph on a separate piece of paper.

CONTRASTING

When you describe the differences between two people, places, or things, you are contrasting them.

Read the model paragraph.

Two Different Restaurants

When my friend Michael was in Sedona last week, he had lunch at Cantina Italiana and dinner at the Cityside Café. The restaurants Cantina Italiana and Cityside Café are different in several ways. First of all, the quality of the food was very different. The food at Cantina was fresh, cooked perfectly, and delicious. On the other hand, food at Cityside was not fresh and it was over-cooked and tasted terrible. The atmosphere at Cantina Italiana was much better than the one at Cityside. Michael thought Cantina was clean and quiet. However, he thought the Cityside Café was dirty and noisy. In addition, while the server at the Cantina Italiana was attentive and polite to Michael, the server at Cityside was inattentive and was rude to him. Finally, although the meal at Cantina was more expensive than the meal at Cityside, it was worth the price. Michael will always remember his delicious lunch at Cantina Italiana, but he can't wait to forget his terrible dinner at Cityside Café.

Make a list of the differences between the two restaurants.

_____   _____

_____   _____

_____   _____

Signal Words of Contrast

English uses special sentence patterns and signal words to show contrast.

Study the chart.

Signal Words of Contrast	Examples
However, *in contrast*, and *on the other hand* are used at the beginning of a sentence to signal to the reader that an idea expressed in that sentence is being contrasted with an idea in the previous sentence. Use a comma after these words and phrases.	In South Africa, red is the color of mourning. **However**, in China, red is the color of good luck. **On the other hand**, in China, red is the color of good luck. **In contrast**, in China, red is the color of good luck.

While, *whereas*, and *but* are used to show contrast between two clauses in one sentence. *While* and *whereas* can be used at the beginning or in the middle of a sentence.	Dr. Meng specializes in surgery, **while** Dr. Becker specializes in internal medicine. Dr. Meng specializes in surgery, **whereas** Dr. Becker specializes in internal medicine. **While** Dr. Becker specializes in internal medicine, Dr. Meng specializes in surgery. **Whereas** Dr. Becker specializes in internal medicine, Dr. Meng specializes in surgery.
But is used in the middle of a sentence. Use a comma to separate the clauses.	Dr. Becker specializes in internal medicine, **but** Dr. Meng specializes in surgery.
Different from and *unlike* are used to show contrast between two nouns. *Different from* is used in the middle of a sentence. *Unlike* is often used to show the same contrast. It is used at the beginning of a sentence.	My mother's personality is **different from** my father's personality. **Unlike** my mother, my father is quiet.

PRACTICE **A** **Read the pairs of sentences. Write three sentences of contrast for each pair. Use the words given.**

1. I am usually punctual. My brother is often late.

   a. (but) *I am usually punctual, but my brother is often late.*

   b. (however) *I am usually punctual. However, my brother is often late.*

   c. (while) *While I am usually punctual, my brother is often late.*

2. In Egypt and Burma, yellow signifies mourning. White means mourning in China and Japan.

   a. (on the other hand) _____

   b. (however) _____

   c. (but) _____

3. In the United States, people drive on the right side of the road. In Turkey, people drive on the left side of the road.

   a. (whereas) _____

   b. (while) _____

   c. (but) _____

4. Some mushrooms are edible and safe to eat. Other mushrooms are poisonous and should be avoided.

   a. (unlike) _____

   b. (whereas) _____

   c. (in contrast) _____

5. Herbivores, such as deer and koalas, only eat plants. Carnivores, such as lions and tigers, only eat meat.

   a. (on the other hand) _____

   b. (while) _____

   c. (unlike) _____

B   **Add signal words that show contrast in the following paragraphs.**

1.

Two Different English Programs

Sunny English Institute (SEI) in Miami, Florida, is _____ Rocky Mountain English Program (RMEP) in Denver, Colorado, in several ways. First of all, the tuition at SEI is very expensive. _____, the tuition at RMEP is more reasonable. Secondly, _____ RMEP is a small school, SEI is a very big school. The program at SEI is two months. _____, the program at RMEP is only five weeks. Finally, SEI includes a TOEFL preparation class, _____ RMEP does not.

2.

Spelling Differences between British English and American English

There are several spelling differences between British English and American English. For example, _____ certain nouns end in -*our* in British English, such as *colour, honour, humour,* and *labour,* these words end in -*or* in American English: *color, honor, humor,* and *labor.* Also, some verbs end in -*ise* in British English, such as *specialise, recognise,* and *patronise.* _____, they end in -*ize* in American English: *specialize, recognize,* and *patronize.*

3.

Vegan or Vegetarian?

A vegan diet and a vegetarian diet are different in several ways. My friend Lily has a very specific diet. She is a vegan. Vegans are much stricter than vegetarians. Naturally, vegans do not eat meat, fish, or poultry. _____ unlike vegetarians like myself, who eat eggs, milk, and butter, vegans do not eat dairy foods or any animal byproducts at all. In fact, some vegans, like Lily, will not even eat honey because it comes from bees, _____ vegetarians who are not vegan usually will. Vegans avoid using products that have been tested on animals. Most vegans, like my friend Lily, love animals and feel that being a vegan is one way to help protect animals. In this way, most vegans and vegetarians are similar.

C Work in groups of four. Complete the chart with information about yourself and the people in your group. Then write sentences that compare or contrast the people in your group.

Names	What is your favorite color?	What is your favorite food?	What is your favorite kind of music?	What sports do you like?
Your name:				

1. _____

2. _____

3. _____

4. _____

5. _____

6. _____

GRAMMAR FOR WRITING: Comparative Adjectives

Adjectives that are used to show the difference between two things are called *comparative adjectives*. Comparative adjectives are often followed by *than*.

Study the rules for writing sentences with comparative adjectives.

RULES	EXAMPLES	SENTENCES
Add *-er* to adjectives that have one syllable. (Note: double the final consonant if it is preceded by a vowel.)	light ⟶ light**er** big ⟶ big**ger**	A feather is **lighter than** a rock. Abu Dhabi is **bigger than** Ajman.
Add *-ier* to adjectives that have two syllables and end in **-y**.	funny ⟶ funn**ier**	My joke is **funnier than** your joke.
Use *more* in front of adjectives that have two or more syllables.	interesting ⟶ **more** interesting	I think biology is **more interesting than** physics.

Notice these common exceptions:

- good ⟶ better
- well ⟶ better
- bad ⟶ worse
- far, farther ⟶ further

Read the paragraph and underline the comparative adjectives.

Different Brothers

Sam and Owen are brothers, but they are different in many ways. For one thing, their physical appearances are very different. Sam is taller and thinner than Owen. Owen has darker eyes and longer hair than Sam. Their personalities are also different. Sam is more serious and more ambitious than Owen. He is a better student because he studies harder than his brother. On the other hand, Owen is more creative and more social than Sam.

PRACTICE **Practice using comparative adjectives. Use the adjective given. Write sentences.**

1. Gary weighs 178 pounds. Gerald weighs 165 pounds. (heavy)

   Gary is heavier than Gerald.

2. The Nile is 4,145 miles long. The Amazon is 3,915 miles long. (long)

   _____

3. The Pacific Ocean is 36,198 feet deep. The Atlantic Ocean is 28,374 feet deep. (deep)

   _____

4. The third chapter is short. The fourth chapter is long. (short)

_____

5. The black dress is $75. The purple dress is $120. (expensive)

_____

6. Mount Everest is 29,025 feet high. Mount Fuji is 12,389 feet high. (high)

_____

7. Traditional college courses meet at a specific time. Online courses meet any time. (convenient)

_____

8. Heavy metal music is loud. Blues music is soft. (loud)

_____

Writing Topic Sentences for Contrast Paragraphs

When you write the topic sentence for a contrast paragraph, you must state the two things that you are contrasting. Look at the following list of sample topic sentences.

- *The Reporter* and *Style* are different types of weekly magazines.
- *The Reporter* and *Style* are different in many ways.
- *The Reporter* and *Style* have many differences.
- *The Reporter* and *Style* differ in several ways.

PRACTICE **A** **Write a topic sentence for each of the following paragraphs.**

1.

Different Cities, Different Weather

_____ First of all, the temperature in Westland is usually hotter than it is in Eastfalls. In Westland it is often in the nineties, but in Eastfalls, the temperature rarely goes above 80. Secondly, the humidity is much higher in Westland than it is in Eastfalls. This makes it much more uncomfortable to be outdoors in Westland. Finally, it rains a lot in Westland. However, it is usually dry in Eastfalls. Overall, the weather in Eastfalls is more pleasant.

2.

Different Sisters

_____ For one thing, they are different in appearance. Florence is short with long, straight, brown hair, but Carmen is tall with short, curly, black hair. Another difference is in their personalities. Florence is very friendly and outgoing. On the other hand, Carmen is shy and quiet. Finally, my two sisters differ in their hobbies. Unlike Florence who loves sports, Carmen likes to spend her free time cooking.

3.

Different Magazines

_____ First of all, *The Reporter* comes out once a week, but *Style* only comes out once a month. Secondly, the two magazines have different sections. *The Reporter* has sections on politics, finance, science, and culture. On the other hand, *Style* has sections on fashion, home decorating, cooking, and gardening. In addition, *The Reporter* is less expensive. It costs $6 per issue, but *Style* costs $8 per issue. Finally, *The Reporter* is available in print and online; however, *Style* is only in available in print.

WRITER'S TIP: Compare and Contrast

When you choose two things to compare or contrast, make sure the two things belong to the same general category. For example, you could compare or contrast two friends, two songs, two types of computers. But you should not compare or contrast cars with computers. You could, however, compare and contrast cars and motorcycles as they belong to the same category: types of transportation.

WRITING PARAGRAPHS OF CONTRAST

Paragraph Practice 1

 Prewriting

A **You and your friend are looking for an apartment to share near campus. You saw these two descriptions of apartments on the Internet. Read the descriptions.**

B Write four sentences contrasting the two apartments.

1. _____

2. _____

3. _____

4. _____

Writing

Which apartment would you choose? Write the first draft of a paragraph explaining your decision and the differences between the two apartments. Include a title.

_____

_____

_____

_____

_____

_____

_____

_____

Revising

A Read your paragraph and look for ways to improve it. Use the Revising Checklist on page 77 to help you.

B Copy your revised paragraph on a separate piece of paper.

Paragraph Practice 2

Prewriting

A You and a friend are planning a trip to Hawaii. You found these advertisements in the newspaper. Read the advertisements.

PLAN A

Hawaiian FLING

Price: **$2599.00**

Length: 8 days, 7 nights

Includes:
Airfare from Los Angeles to Honolulu
Welcome party
Visit two islands: Waikiki and Oahu
Breakfast and dinner
Three-star hotel accommodations
Transportation to and from airport

PLAN B

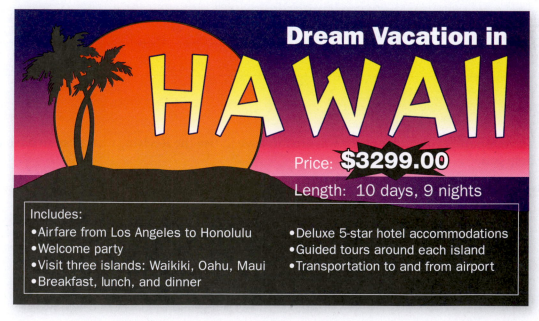

Dream Vacation in HAWAII

Price: **$3299.00**

Length: 10 days, 9 nights

Includes:
- Airfare from Los Angeles to Honolulu
- Welcome party
- Visit three islands: Waikiki, Oahu, Maui
- Breakfast, lunch, and dinner
- Deluxe 5-star hotel accommodations
- Guided tours around each island
- Transportation to and from airport

B Make a list of differences between the two trips.

_____   _____

_____   _____

_____   _____

_____   _____

 Writing

Write a one-paragraph email message to your friend contrasting the two plans and suggesting the one you think would be better for you.

To: mypal@anyschool.edu
From:
Subject: Hawaii trip

Revising

A Read your email and look for ways to improve it.

B Copy your revised email on a separate piece of paper.

Paragraph Practice 3

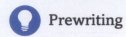 **Prewriting**

A Talk to a classmate from another country. Discuss the differences between your two cultures. If everyone in the class is from the same country, discuss the differences between your family and your partner's family. Discuss these topics.

- eating habits
- climate
- social customs

- family life
- education
- political system

B Choose one of the topics to write about. Make a list of the differences.

_____   _____

_____   _____

_____   _____

C Write a topic sentence. Include the topic (education, family life, etc.) you are contrasting and the names of the two countries.

Example:

There are several differences in social customs between Peru and Taiwan.

_____

Writing

Write the first draft of a paragraph of contrast. Use your list as a guide. Start with the biggest differences. Include a title.

_____

_____

_____

_____

_____

_____

_____

_____

_____

 **Revising**

A Exchange paragraphs with a partner. Ask your partner for suggestions to improve your paragraph and give suggestions to improve your partner's paragraph. You can also use the Revising Checklist on page 77 to help you.

B Copy your revised paragraph on a separate piece of paper.

YOU BE THE EDITOR

The email message has ten mistakes. Correct the mistakes. Copy the corrected message on a separate piece of paper.

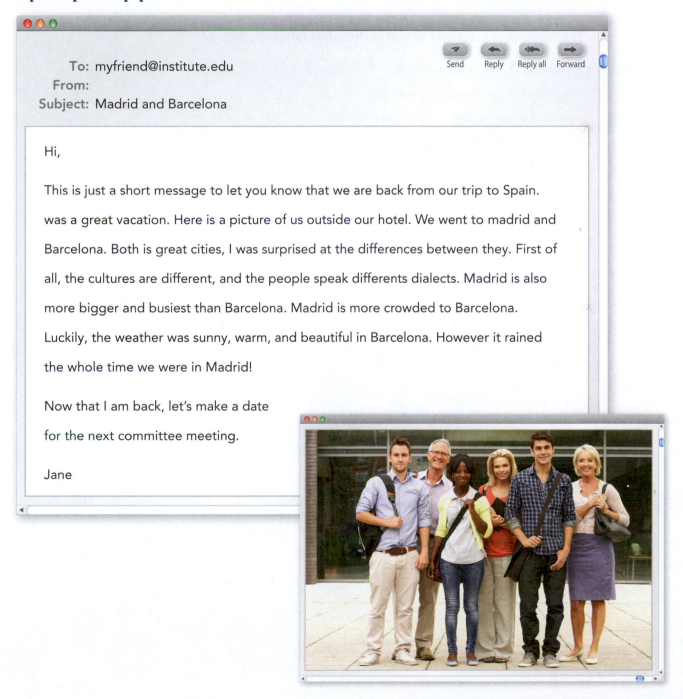

To: myfriend@institute.edu
From:
Subject: Madrid and Barcelona

Hi,

This is just a short message to let you know that we are back from our trip to Spain. was a great vacation. Here is a picture of us outside our hotel. We went to madrid and Barcelona. Both is great cities, I was surprised at the differences between they. First of all, the cultures are different, and the people speak differents dialects. Madrid is also more bigger and busiest than Barcelona. Madrid is more crowded to Barcelona. Luckily, the weather was sunny, warm, and beautiful in Barcelona. However it rained the whole time we were in Madrid!

Now that I am back, let's make a date for the next committee meeting.

Jane

ON YOUR OWN

(A) **Choose one of the following topics to write about. You may write about either the similarities or the differences.**

- two cities you have visited
- two vacations you have taken
- two jobs you have had
- two athletic teams you like
- two types of music
- an online course and a traditional course

(B) **Write a paragraph comparing Benjamin Franklin and Thomas Jefferson. Use the information that follows as well as the information on page 177.**

Benjamin Franklin 1706–1790

- founded University of Pennsylvania
- helped write Declaration of Independence
- important person in American Revolution
- well-known philosopher and thinker
- ambassador to France

CHAPTER 12 Analyzing Causes and Effects

....
LEARNING OUTCOME
....
Paragraph Writing: Write a paragraph describing the causes or effects of an event

Most situations, events, and actions have causes and effects. For example, when you explain *why* something happened, or *why* you made a certain decision, you are describing the causes or reasons. On the other hand, when you explain the results of something that happened, or the results of a decision you made, you are describing the effects. In this chapter, you will learn how to write about the causes and effects of a situation.

WRITING ABOUT CAUSES

Read the model paragraph. Circle the topic sentence. Underline the three main reasons the student gives for taking a year off from college.

A Year Off

I've decided to take a year off from college for several reasons. First of all, I need to work for a while because the tuition has gone up. Paying the tuition and living in the dorm is very expensive. I know I can save money by living at home and working. In addition, I need time away from school to think about my major. Since I'm not really sure what career path I want to pursue, I don't want to waste time and money taking the wrong courses. Most importantly, I just need a break from the stress of school. I was feeling a lot of pressure to get high grades and excel at everything at school. I was also getting headaches and stomachaches due to all the stress. I didn't make my decision lightly, but I hope it is the right one.

Look at the sets of pictures. The first picture in each set shows a cause. The second picture shows an effect. Write a sentence that describes each picture.

1. Cause: ___The man found $100.___   Effect: ___He is happy.___

2. Cause: _____   Effect: _____

_____   _____

3. Cause: _____   Effect: _____

_____   _____

4. Cause: _____   Effect: _____

_____   _____

GRAMMAR FOR WRITING: Complex Sentences with *Because* and *Since*

You have learned that a **complex sentence** is formed by joining an independent clause with a dependent clause. Remember that an **independent clause** is like a simple sentence. It has a subject and a verb, and it expresses a complete thought. A **dependent clause** also has a subject and a verb, but it does not express a complete thought. A dependent clause always begins with a **subordinating conjunction**. Two important subordinating conjunctions that express cause are *because* and *since*.

Study the chart.

Subordinating Conjunctions: *Because* and *Since*	Examples
Because and *since* have similar meaning and are used the same way. They both introduce a dependent clause that states a reason or cause for something. The cause clause can come at the beginning of a sentence. Use a comma if the clause that begins with *because* or *since* comes at the beginning of a sentence. The cause clause can also come at the end of a sentence without changing the meaning of the sentence. Notice that the independent clause explains the result.	Amanda got to work late **because** she missed the bus. Amanda got to work late **since** she missed the bus. 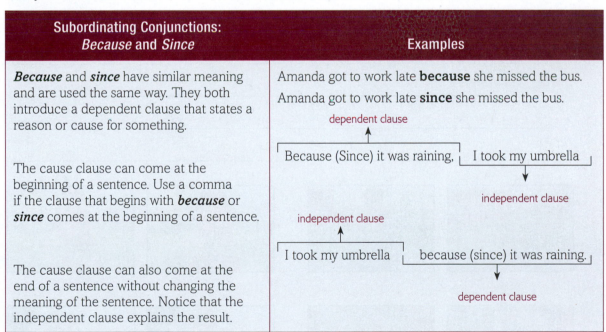

Read the sentences. Circle the subordinating conjunctions *because* or *since* in each sentence. Then underline the dependent clause (the cause) once and the independent clause (the result) twice.

1. I took a long nap this afternoon because I was so tired.

2. Since Barry memorized all the vocabulary words, he got a perfect score on the quiz.

3. Because we followed the directions, we got to the restaurant without getting lost.

4. I had to borrow my friend's dictionary because I left mine at home.

5. Since it is so windy today, we postponed our badminton game.

B   **Complete the complex sentences.**

1. I took an aspirin because _____

2. Because it is snowing, _____

3. Since it is very hot today, _____

4. _____ since I have a big exam tomorrow.

5. Because Ari drank too much coffee, _____

6. Since I ate too much for lunch, _____

7. _____ I got to school early.

C   **Write a complex sentence of cause for each of the sets of pictures. Use *because*.**

1. *The boy is happy because he found $100.* _____

2. _____

3. _____

4. _____

JUST FOR FUN

Work with a partner. The questions in column A are all jokes. Match the questions with the answers in column B. Then write a sentence for each one using *because* or *since*.

A	**B**
_____ 1. Why did the man cross the street?	**a.** Its head is so far from its body.
_____ 2. Why did the man throw the clock out the window?	**b.** They live in schools.
	c. He wanted to see time fly.
_____ 3. Why does the giraffe have such a long neck?	**d.** He wanted to get to the other side.
_____ 4. Why did the man tiptoe past the medicine cabinet?	**e.** He didn't want to wake up the sleeping pills.
_____ 5. Why are fish smarter than insects?	**f.** It has the largest number of stories.
_____ 6. Why is a library the tallest building?	

1. _____

2. _____

3. _____

4. _____

5. _____

6. _____

Signal Words of Cause

You have already seen how *because* and *since* introduce clauses of cause or reason. *Due to* and *Because of* also introduce causes and reasons, but they introduce phrases instead of clauses.

Study the chart.

Signal Words that Introduce Causes	Examples
Due to and *because of* introduce a noun phrase that states a cause. The cause phrase can come in the middle of the sentence.	I took my umbrella **due to the rain.** I took my umbrella **because of the rain.**
The cause phrase can come at the beginning of a sentence, too. Use a comma if the phrase that begins with *because of* or *due to* comes at the beginning of a sentence.	**Because of the rain,** I took my umbrella. **Due to the rain,** I took my umbrella.

Complete the sentences.

1. _____ because of the fire.

2. Due to the drought, _____

3. _____ because of the crisis in the economy.

4. Due to my stressful job, _____

5. _____ because of the loud noise. _____

6. _____ due to the high rate of unemployment.

7. Due to her hard work, _____

8. _____ because of the snowstorm.

Writing Topic Sentences for Paragraphs about Cause and Effect

When you write a paragraph about cause and effect, your topic sentence should identify the effect (the situation, decision, event, etc.) and the number of causes. You can use expressions such as *several reasons*, *three main causes*, *two major reasons*.

Here are some examples of topic sentences for paragraphs about cause and effect.

Examples:

*I decided to move to New York **for several reasons**.*

*The economy is doing well **for three main reasons**.*

***There are several causes** of diabetes in adults.*

PRACTICE **Write topic sentences for the following paragraphs.**

1.
Why People Move

_____ Some people move because they want to find better jobs or to advance their careers. Others are attracted to new places because of better weather. Still others want to move to a place with less crime. Finally, people often want to move to a place with a lower cost of living. For these reasons, every year millions of people pack up and move to new places.

2.
Overweight Children

_____ One reason so many American children are overweight is that they eat too much junk food that is high in calories, sugar, and fat. Another reason is that many children do not get enough exercise. Because they spend so much time sitting in front of the television set or playing computer games, they do not move around very much. Genetics is another reason that children become overweight. Children whose parents or brothers or sisters are overweight may be at an increased risk of becoming overweight themselves.

3.

A Winning Team

_____ First of all, our soccer team had a great coach. He inspired us to play our best and gave us a lot of helpful advice. Another reason we won the tournament was due to our loyal fans. They came to all of our games and cheered us on. Without their support we probably wouldn't have won. Most importantly, we owe our success to our team spirit. Because we worked and practiced hard as a team, we were able to achieve our goal and win the tournament.

4.

A Difficult Language

_____ One reason is that the English spelling system is very irregular. Many words sound the same but are spelled differently. For example, *hear* and *here* sound the same but are spelled differently. In addition, many of the grammar rules are complicated. For every rule it seems that there are two exceptions. Finally, English is difficult to master because of the many idioms. In fact, native speakers commonly use more than 8,000 idioms!

WRITING PARAGRAPHS ABOUT CAUSES

Paragraph Practice 1

Prewriting

Over the past 150 years there has been a huge increase in population. Read the list of causes and discuss them in small groups.

- advances in medicine and health care
- better sanitation
- improved farming methods that produce more and better food
- fewer infant deaths and more people living longer

Writing

Use the list to write a paragraph about the causes of the population increase. Begin with a topic sentence and include signal words. Add a title.

_____

_____

_____

_____

_____

_____

_____

Revising

A Read the paragraph you wrote. Look for ways to improve it. Use the Revising Checklist on page 77 to help you.

B Copy your revised paragraph on a separate piece of paper.

Paragraph Practice 2

Prewriting

A Think of an important decision you have made, or choose one of the following:

- getting married
- choosing your major
- accepting or quitting a job
- buying a house
- moving to another country
- having a baby

B Why did you make your decision? Make a list of reasons that influenced your decision.

_____   _____

_____   _____

C Write a topic sentence for your paragraph.

_____

Writing

Write the first draft of your paragraph. Use your list of reasons as a guide. Include a title.

_____

_____

_____

_____

_____

_____

_____

_____

_____

Revising

(A) Exchange paragraphs with a classmate. Give each other suggestions for improving your paragraphs. You can use the Revising Checklist on page 77 to help you.

(B) Use your partner's ideas to improve your paragraph. Also, consider these questions.

1. Do all of your reasons relate to the decision stated in the topic sentence?

2. Are your reasons in a logical order? Did you include signal words?

3. Did you clearly identify the causes and effects? Did you use words like *because* and *since*?

(C) Copy your revised paragraph on a separate piece of paper.

Paragraph Practice 3

Prewriting

Situation: You are a business administration student. You have been asked to analyze the following case from 1998.

(A) Read the case.

> **CASE #6**
>
> On September 5, 1998, Michael Williams opened a small music store selling compact discs. The store is located next to the lobby on the ground floor of the Fairfax Apartment Building. The apartment building is on a small side street just outside of town. It is 3 miles away from a shopping center that has two large music stores.
>
> Mr. Williams spent $15,000 buying CDs for his shop. Most of the CDs were hip-hop and rock. He sold each CD for $15. He hired two people to work as sales clerks and paid them $8.50 an hour. The shop was open Monday to Friday from 1 to 5 P.M. Mr. Williams would not accept checks or credit cards.
>
> On December 19, 1999, Mr. Williams closed his shop. He put a sign on the door that said "Out of Business."

(B) Discuss this case in your group. Why do you think the business failed? Make a list of at least four causes. You can add more later.

_____

_____

_____

_____

_____

C Now study this graph and answer the questions.

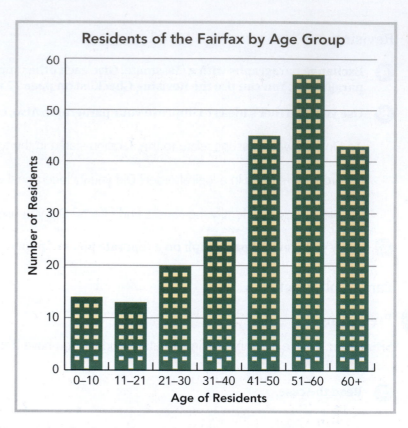

Residents of the Fairfax by Age Group

Number of Residents (y-axis: 0 to 60)

Age of Residents (x-axis): 0–10, 11–21, 21–30, 31–40, 41–50, 51–60, 60+

1. How would you describe the people who live in the Fairfax? What generalization can you make about the people?

_____

_____

_____

2. Can you use the information in this graph to think of another cause of the failure of this business? Add it to your list of causes on page 201.

D Now study the following table. Write three statements based on the table.

NUMBER OF PEOPLE WHO WALK PAST THE STORE						
	MON	TUES	WED	THURS	FRI	SAT	SUN
8 A.M.–12 P.M.	30	35	28	29	31	32	20
12 P.M.–6 P.M.	10	12	16	15	20	70	65
6 P.M.–12 A.M.	40	47	53	42	60	65	40

1. _____

2. _____

3. _____

E The information in this table shows another cause of the failure. What is it? Add it to your list of causes on page 201.

F Look over your list of causes. Can you think of any others? Are there any you want to cross out?

 Writing

With your group, write the first draft of a paragraph explaining the failure of Mr. Williams's music shop. Include a title.

_____

_____

_____

_____

_____

_____

_____

_____

_____

_____

Revising

A Read your paragraph and look for ways to improve it. Use the Revising Checklist on page 77 to help you. Also, think about these questions.

1. Do all of your causes help explain why Mr. Williams's compact disc shop failed?

2. Are your causes in a logical order?

3. Did you include signal words?

4. Did you clearly identify the causes and effects? Did you use words like *because* and *since*?

B Copy your revised paragraph on a separate piece of paper.

WRITING ABOUT EFFECTS

Read the model paragraph. Underline the topic sentence and answer the questions that follow.

Taking a salsa dance class has had many positive effects on my life. One of the first things I noticed was the physical effect. As a result of taking this class, I am in much better shape. For example, my posture and coordination are better. Salsa dancing requires a lot of physical energy and burns a lot of calories, so I've lost several pounds. Another effect is that I have more self-confidence. Consequently, my social skills have improved, and I've become more outgoing. Finally, I've met a lot of great people taking salsa classes. This leads to the biggest effect on my life. I'm engaged to marry a great guy that I met in the class!

1. What effects does the author give?

_____

_____

2. What was the biggest effect?

_____

Signal Words That Show Effects

English uses special sentence patterns and signal words to express effects.

Study the chart.

Signal Words that Introduce Effects	Examples
We use *therefore*, *thus*, *consequently*, and *as a result* to show a *cause and effect* relationship between two complete sentences. These words introduce the effect, which is always stated in the second sentence. Use a comma after these words.	Our company is expanding rapidly. **Therefore,** we hired more people. Our company is expanding rapidly. **Consequently,** we hired more people. Our company is expanding rapidly. **As a result,** we hired more people. Our company is expanding rapidly. **Thus,** we hired more people.
We also use *so* to show a *cause and effect* relationship. *So* combines two simple sentences into one compound sentence. Use a comma before *so*.	Our company is expanding rapidly, **so** we hired more people.

A Write a sentence of cause and effect for each of the sets of pictures on pages 194–195. Use *therefore* in the first two sentences. Use *so* in the last two sentences.

1. *The young man found $100. Therefore, he is happy.*

2. _____

3. _____

4. _____

B Match the effects with their causes.

Effects	**Causes**
_d_ 1. I'm going skiing today.	a. It was faster than the train.
____ 2. We moved to the country.	b. He likes to get exercise in the morning.
____ 3. We bought a new car.	c. The city was too crowded.
____ 4. They took an airplane.	d. It snowed five inches last night.
____ 5. She doesn't eat desserts.	e. It didn't rain enough this summer.
____ 6. The flowers in our garden died.	f. The old one used too much gas.
____ 7. We turned on the air conditioner.	g. She's on a diet.
____ 8. He rides his bike to work.	h. It is very hot today.

C Now combine the causes and effects to make new sentences. Use *thus, consequently, as a result, therefore,* or *so.*

1. *It snowed five inches last night, so I'm going skiing today.*

2. _____

3. _____

4. _____

5. _____

6. _____

7. _____

8. _____

Writing Topic Sentences for Paragraphs about Effects

The topic sentence for a paragraph about effects should state the situation, decision, or event and indicate that you will be discussing its effects. Study the examples.

- *Computers have had several important effects on society.*
- *There are a number of consequences of global warming.*
- *The birth of my twins has had several effects on my life.*
- *The flood caused several problems in our town.*

PRACTICE **Write topic sentences for the following paragraphs.**

1.

Snowstorm Causes Problem

_____ For one thing, there was so much snow that it was dangerous to drive. Most of the side streets were impassable, and several main roads had to be closed. Even the mail was delayed. Students had the day off because all the schools in the area were closed. Many stores and businesses were closed as well. Finally, the snowstorm cost the city a lot of money to remove the snow and plow the roads.

2.

Benefits of Running

_____ First of all, running on a regular basis benefits your body. For example, it can increase the efficiency of your heart and lungs. Running also helps the body develop greater physical endurance. It enables your body to become more mechanically efficient and can improve your physical coordination. Finally, running has psychological benefits. It can improve your mood and lower your stress level.

3.

Music for Children

_____ Some studies show that listening to music can increase a child's verbal and emotional intelligence. It can also improve concentration and stimulate creative thinking. Some scientists think music can even improve children's memory. Finally, music can relax children and make them feel more comfortable. Overall, it seems that music is beneficial to children's learning and sense of well-being.

IRRELEVANT SENTENCES

PRACTICE **The following paragraphs each contain one sentence that is irrelevant. Cross out that sentence. Then explain to a partner why it does not belong.**

1.

Waiting to Have Children

There are several reasons why many American women are waiting until they are thirty years old or older to have their first baby. Some women have good jobs and want to continue their careers. Many American couples have two children. Other women don't want the responsibility of having children until they are older. Still others are waiting until they are financially secure before they start a family. Increased personal and professional opportunities for women often result in delaying motherhood.

2.

The Positive Effects of Watching Television

Watching television can have several positive effects on students learning English. One effect is that students can improve their pronunciation by listening to the people talking on television. Many commercials are too long and interrupt interesting shows. In addition, students see how native speakers interact while they are talking. As a result, they can observe the gestures and natural body language that are part of communication. Most importantly, because the people on TV use so many idioms, students will hear them used in context. This will help students better understand the meanings of idioms.

3.

> ### The Effects of Affordable Automobiles on Society
>
> The introduction of affordable automobiles had several effects on society. First of all, automobiles created a more mobile society. Cars made it possible for people to move out of the cities and into the suburbs. Automobiles also affected the growth of new businesses. Gas stations, auto repair shops, and roadside restaurants became necessary. Railroads had a great effect on society, too. In addition, new roads were built as a result of the increase in the number of cars. All of these changes meant that the automobile transformed the lifestyle of millions of people.

WRITING PARAGRAPHS ABOUT EFFECTS

Paragraph Practice 1

Prewriting

A **Think about this topic:** There are several effects of global warming.

B **What effects can you and your classmates think of? Brainstorm a list of effects. Your teacher will write them in list form on the board. Copy the list here.**

_____   _____

_____   _____

_____   _____

C **After you have a complete list of effects, discuss them. Decide which should be included in the paragraph. Cross out the ones that are not the most important or relevant effects.**

Writing

Write the first draft of a paragraph about the effects of global warming. Include a title.

_____

_____

_____

_____

_____

_____

_____

_____

🔍 Revising

Ⓐ Read your paragraph and look for ways to improve it. Use the Revising Checklist on page 77 to help you.

Ⓑ Copy the final draft on a separate piece of paper.

Paragraph Practice 2

💡 Prewriting

Discuss this information with a partner.

Drinking a moderate amount of caffeine probably won't cause you any harm. But drinking too much caffeine can have negative effects on your health. Heavy caffeine use is more than 500 to 600 mg a day (four to seven cups of coffee). Here are some of the effects of too much caffeine.

- insomnia
- nervousness, anxiety
- nausea or other gastrointestinal problems

- fast or irregular heartbeat
- muscle tremors
- headaches

✒️ Writing

Use the list to write the first draft of a paragraph about the effects of too much caffeine on the human body. Begin with a topic sentence. Include a title.

_____

_____

_____

_____

_____

_____

_____

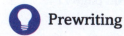 **Revising**

A Read your paragraph and look for ways to improve it. Use the Revising Checklist on page 77 to help you.

B Copy the final draft on a separate piece of paper.

Paragraph Practice 3

 Prewriting

A Read the information.

Acton is a small town in the Midwest of the U.S. It has a population of 2,500. It is a safe, quiet, and clean place to live. Most of the people have lived there all their lives and know each other very well. The town has not changed very much in the past 100 years.

Last month, Stanley Manufacturing decided to open a large factory in Acton. This will bring many new people to the community. Some people are worried about the negative effects the new factory will have on the town. Other people are excited about the positive effects the new factory will have.

B In small groups, make predictions about the impact the new factory will have on Acton. Make a list of all the possible effects you can think of.

Positive Effects	Negative Effects
more jobs	pollution

Writing

Choose one of the following groups.

1. You are part of a group of conservative residents that doesn't want Acton to change. On a separate piece of paper, write a paragraph predicting the negative effects the factory will have on the town.

2. You are a member of a group of progressive residents that is open to changes in your community. On a separate piece of paper, write a paragraph predicting the positive effects the new factory will have on the town.

Revising

A Read over your group's paragraph and look for ways to improve it. Use the Revising Checklist on page 77 to help you.

B Copy your revised paragraph on a separate piece of paper.

Paragraph Practice 4

💡 **Prewriting**

A   **Choose a topic and list the effects of that decision on your life.**

- getting married
- picking a school
- choosing a career
- buying a house
- coming to an
  English-speaking country

_____ _____

_____ _____

_____ _____

_____ _____

_____ _____

B   **Look over your list. Cross out the ideas that are not effects of the decision. Number the effects in order of importance.**

✒️ **Writing**

Write the first draft of your paragraph, using your list as a guide.

_____

_____

_____

_____

_____

_____

_____

🔍 **Revising**

A   **Exchange paragraphs with a classmate. Give each other suggestions for improving your paragraphs. You can use the Revising Checklist on page 77 to help you.**

B   **Copy your revised paragraph on a separate piece of paper.**

YOU BE THE EDITOR

Read the article. It contains nine mistakes. Correct the mistakes. Copy the corrected article on a separate piece of paper.

SURPRISE TORNADO

August 3.

The tornado that hit kansas today surprised even the weather forecasters. the strong winds blew over 200 miles per hour. As a result many crops were destroyed. Hundreds of people lost his homes or offices. Because of the high winds and heavy rain. The Red Cross estimates that the violent tornado caused many injury. Also, millions of dollars worth of farm animals were killed due of the tornado. will take the people of Kansas a long time to recover from the effects of this tornado.

ON YOUR OWN

Choose one of these topics and write a paragraph.
- causes or effects of immigrating to a new country
- causes or effects of stress at work, home, or school
- reasons you decided to learn English
- the effects of forest fires or deforestation
- the reasons you chose your major
- the effects of a teacher or coach on your life
- the reasons so many people shop online

CHAPTER 13 › Writing Summaries and Answering Test Questions

Paragraph writing: Write a paragraph that summarizes an article or a story

Summaries require a special kind of writing. A good summary gives only main ideas. It does not include details. Before you begin to write a summary, you need to read the article or story several times to make sure you understand it completely.

DISTINGUISHING BETWEEN MAIN IDEAS AND DETAILS

Read the article twice. Underline the main ideas during the second reading.

*Local Dog Saves the Day**

A young couple in Halifax County, North Carolina cannot thank an unusual friend enough. The special friend, a black, brown, and white Australian Shepherd named Bosco, saved the day when he saved their little boy.

Three-year-old Owen Parker was visiting his grandparents at their home while his parents were at work. Owen was playing outside in the yard when he wandered off.

Owen's grandfather realized that the boy was missing and immediately began to look for him. He called for the one person he knew would be with Owen. "Bosco! Bosco!" he yelled. But Bosco didn't come running. Bosco was missing, too.

The grandfather's home is next to a huge wooded area where it is easy to get lost. When Owen's grandfather could not find him, he called Owen's dad. Owen's parents rushed right home. A search team was quickly organized. The search team included a police helicopter, police dogs, and many neighbors and volunteers. As soon as news of the missing boy was posted on the Internet, hundreds more people came to help with the search. It was early afternoon, and they hoped to find the boy before evening when it would get dark and cold.

As time went by, Owen's parents became increasingly frightened, but they knew Bosco had to be with Owen and would not leave him alone for long. Australian Shepherds are well known as guard dogs and for their loyalty to their owners. The Parker's got Bosco as a puppy, and raised him alongside Owen. Owen and Bosco had always been best friends.

Several hours passed and it was getting dark. Then, some members of the search team saw Bosco. He was running back and forth in front of a cave near the Parkers' home. They heard Bosco barking loudly. It seemed like the dog was trying to signal them. They rushed toward Bosco who led them to the cave and disappeared inside. When the rescuers went inside, they found Owen safe and sound, asleep on his jacket, with Bosco by his side.

Owens's parents think that Bosco saved their young son. Without Bosco, the search team may never have found the boy in time. As a reward, the Parkers bought Bosco the biggest steak they could find.

*This story is fictional, but based on real events.

A **Read the statements about the story "Local Dog Saves the Day." Write *MI* next to sentences that are main ideas. Write *D* next to sentences that give details.**

_____ 1. Owen's grandparents live near the woods.

_____ 2. Owen's parents were at work.

_____ 3. Owen wandered into the woods, and no one could find him.

_____ 4. Bosco saved Owen's life when he stayed with him and led the search team to him.

_____ 5. Australian Shepherds are well known as guard dogs.

_____ 6. A search team was organized to look for Owen.

_____ 7. Owen was found asleep in a cave near his grandparents' home.

_____ 8. News of Owen's disappearance was posted on the Internet.

_____ 9. A helicopter was used to search the woods.

_____ 10. Bosco received a steak as a reward.

B **Complete the following summary. Use the words in parentheses to help you complete the sentences in the summary.**

_____, (who) a three-year-old boy from _____ (where) wandered into the woods _____ (where) and was missing for several hours. A large search team was organized and tried _____ (what). _____ (when) members of the search team finally saw and heard the Parker's dog, Bosco. They followed Bosco and discovered Owen sleeping in a cave. Bosco is hailed as a _____ (what) because _____ (why).

GRAMMAR FOR WRITING: Agreement of Subjects and Verbs

Every English sentence must have a subject and a verb. In order for a sentence to be grammatically correct, the subject and verb must agree with each other in number. This means that when the subject is singular, the verb must be singular. When the subject is plural, the verb must be plural.

Example:

My **sister lives** in Michigan. (Singular subject and singular verb)

My **sisters live** in Michigan. (Plural subject and plural verb.)

Study the chart.

Rule	Examples
Singular subjects take singular verbs.	My **roommate takes** violin lessons. The new **student is** from Turkey.
Plural subjects take plural verbs. When subjects (singular or plural) are joined by **and**, they are considered plural.	The new **students are** from Turkey. My **roommate** *and* **I were** early for class.
If the subjects of a sentence are joined with **or** the verb should agree with the subject closest to the verb. Use a singular verb if the subject closer to the verb is singular. Use a plural verb if the subject closer to the verb is plural. Sentences with subjects joined with **or** often begin with **either**. Negative sentences often join subjects with **nor** or **neither . . . nor**. As with **or**, the verb agrees in number with the subject close to it.	Nancy *or* **her roommate drives** to school every day. Nancy *or* **her roommates drive** to school every day. **Either** Nancy **or** her roommates drive to school every day. Ann **nor** *her sisters eat* lunch in the cafeteria. **Neither** my sisters **nor** *Ann wants* to join the chess club.
The verb should agree with its subject, not with the words that come between. For example, if a prepositional phrase comes between the subject and verb, the verb still agrees with the subject and not the words in between.	My favorite **book** of short stories **is** by Edgar Allen Poe. The **stories** in this book **are** by Edgar Allen Poe.
Use a singular verb with expressions of time, money, measurement, weight, and fractions.	**Three minutes was** all the time we needed to answer the questions, **Thirty dollars is** a good price for this sweatshirt.

PRACTICE **Circle the correct verb in each of the following sentences.**

1. My friends (likes / like) to go to concerts on the weekends.

2. The new teacher (don't / doesn't) give a lot of homework.

3. Fifty dollars (is / are) too much to spend on dinner at this restaurant.

4. The book and the movie (has / have) different endings.

5. The first question on the exam (was / were) easy.

6. The second and third questions on the exam (was / were) difficult.

7. The new students (sits / sit) in the front row.

8. The new book by Joan and David Thompson (is / are) very interesting.

9. The woman with three young children (go / goes) to the park every afternoon.

10. Either Jason or his lab partners (write / writes) the lab report.

11. Neither my brothers nor my sister (enjoy / enjoys) classical music.

GRAMMAR FOR WRITING: Verb and Pronoun Agreement

Some subject pronouns always take singular verbs. Some subject pronouns always take plural verbs.

Study the chart

Singular Pronouns				Examples
Use a singular verb with these pronouns.				**Everybody wants** smaller classes. (*Everybody* is the subject.)
anyone	everybody	neither	no one	**Everything** in this box **belongs** to me. (*Everybody* is the subject.)
anything	everyone	somebody	nobody	
each	everything	someone	none	**One** of my friends **is** moving to Colorado. (*One* is the subject.)
either	one	something	nothing	

Plural Pronouns			Examples
Use a plural verb with these pronouns.			**Several** of the students **need** help with their projects. (*Several* is the subject.)
both	few	many	
others	several		**Others want** more breaks. (*Others* is the subject.)

PRACTICE **Circle the correct verb in each of the following sentences.**

1. One of my cousins (has / have) a new laptop.

2. Everyone who does the homework (get / gets) a good grade.

3. Most of my classmates (like / likes) the English professor.

4. One of the reasons that I decided to be a teacher (is / are) that I like to work with people.

5. Both Hyun and her cousin (study / studies) medicine at the University of Pennsylvania Medical School.

6. Everyone on the team (comes / come) to soccer practice every afternoon.

7. All the team members (has / have) new uniforms.

8. Each one of your children (is / are) getting taller.

9. He said, "Nobody (cares / care) about the entrance exam."

10. Someone (is / are) going to arrange the flowers for the party.

WRITING A SUMMARY

The hardest part of writing a summary is deciding what to include and what to leave out. It will help if you think about answering the questions *Who?*, *When?*, *Where?*, *Why?*, *What?*, and *How?* in your summary. Remember to include only the author's opinions and ideas, not your own opinions. But remember to use your own words. If you use the author's words, you need to put them in quotations.

Paragraph Practice 1

 Prewriting

Read the story. Discuss it with your classmates.

> ### The Sweetest Melody
> #### A Folk Tale from Afghanistan
>
> Long ago, there lived a shah (king) of Persia named Abbas who was clever and wise. He was curious about the world and often asked riddles. One day the shah was talking to four of his advisers, discussing music and art and life. Suddenly the shah asked, "What is the sweetest melody?"
>
> The first adviser immediately answered, "Without question, the melody of the flute is the sweetest. It sounds like a bird singing in a tree." The second adviser spoke up. "No, no, you have it all wrong. The melody of the harp is by far the sweetest. It sounds as beautiful as the music that is played in heaven." Then the third adviser said, "You are both wrong. In all of the universe, the melody of the violin has the most pleasing sound. It can play loudly and boldly. It can play softly and sweetly. When a man hears it, he feels like someone is strumming his own heart."

The first three advisers argued bitterly. But the fourth adviser, Zaki, just watched quietly. Finally, the other three advisers looked at Shah Abbas to find out which of them was right. But the shah was looking at Zaki, who was the wisest of them all. But still he said nothing. He just sat there listening without offering his opinion. Then, the shah sent them all from the room.

Several days passed. Then, Zaki invited Shah Abbas and the other advisers to a banquet in their honor. That evening, the best and most renowned musicians in the land played all kinds of instruments, including the flute, harp, and violin. The music was exquisite, but there was no food on the table. "How strange," the advisers noticed. "There is a table here but no food." Usually at these banquets, the tables would be filled with all kinds of food. Even after guests had finished eating, the waiters would keep bringing out more and more food.

But this night was different. Although the music was plentiful, the table was empty. Where was the food? The guests' stomachs began to rumble with hunger. They looked around hopefully for the great dishes of meat and rice they expected. "We've been here for hours!" they thought to themselves. "We will starve." It was nearly midnight, and still they waited. Finally, Zaki called for the waiter. The waiter brought an enormous pot of hot food into the room. Zaki lifted the metal lid off the pot and hit it with a silver spoon. "Clung! Clung!" The sound rang through the silent room like a great bell.

All the guests smiled in relief. The wise adviser smiled at the shah and said, "The sound of food to a hungry man—that is the sweetest melody!" Suddenly, the shah spoke up in excitement. "Yes," he said to Zaki. "That is the answer."

 Writing

Work with a partner. Complete the summary of "The Sweetest Melody."

"The Sweetest Melody" is a story about _____

_____.

One day the shah asked _____, "What is _____?"

Three of the advisers gave different answers. The first answered _____

_____.

The second said _____,

and the third said _____.

They argued, but Zaki, the fourth and wisest adviser, didn't answer. _____,

Zaki invited the shah and his advisers to a banquet. There were many musicians, but there was

no food on the table. As the night continued, the guests got _____.

_____, a waiter brought in a big pot of food.

Zaki hit the lid of the pot with a large spoon. Then he smiled and said, "The sound of food to a

hungry man—_____!"

 **Revising**

Work in a group. Compare your summaries.

Paragraph Practice 2

 **Prewriting**

A Read the following section from an ecology textbook. Read it the first time for the main idea. Then read it a second time and underline the main points.

Why Do Some Animals Die Out?

It is natural for species of animals to become extinct over millions of years. But, over the past 200 years, humans have caused the process to speed up. In recent years, the total number of threatened animal species has increased from 5,205 to 5,435. Today 25 percent (one in four) of mammal species and 12 percent (one in eight) of bird species are threatened with extinction. In most cases, this is a result of human activity. How are people accelerating the process of animal extinction?

First of all, people threaten the survival of animal species by destroying their habitats. As human populations grow, people keep building houses and factories in fields and woods. As they spread over the land, they destroy animals' homes. If the animals can't find a place to live, they die out. Twenty-three kinds of Hawaiian birds have become extinct for this reason. Other animals, such as the Florida Key deer, may soon die out because they are losing their homes.

Overhunting is another way that humans are causing some animals to become extinct. In some parts of the world, the parts of rare animals are worth a lot of money. For example, some people will pay more than $1,000 for a single rhino horn. This encourages hunters to kill rhinos even though the animal faces extinction. Other animals that are threatened with extinction from overhunting include the blue whale, the mountain gorilla, and the cheetah.

Humans are also polluting the air, water, and soil. The effect of pollution on animal species can be complicated. For example, when waste from factories is dumped into rivers, the rivers become polluted. The fish that live in the river are poisoned and many of them die. In addition, birds that eat the poisoned fish become poisoned themselves. Once they are poisoned, these birds cannot lay strong, healthy eggs. Fewer and fewer new birds are born. So far, no animals have become extinct because of pollution. But some, such as the brown pelican, became rare and almost died out.

Finally, when humans introduce new species into certain environments, the animals that already live there become threatened and face extinction. For example, when European settlers brought rabbits and foxes to Australia, they killed off many native Australian animals, including the bandicoot. The rabbits and foxes adapted to the Australian environment very quickly and multiplied rapidly. Eventually, the foxes hunted and killed many bandicoots for food. The rabbits took over the bandicoot habitats. Now the bandicoots are threatened with extinction in their own land.

B Now answer the following questions.

1. What is the section about?

   _____

2. What is happening?

   _____

3. Why is this happening?

   _____

4. Where is this happening?

   _____

5. Who is responsible?

   _____

6. When is it happening?

   _____

Writing

Write the first draft of your summary. Remember to include a topic sentence that states the main idea. Add supporting sentences that explain, in your own words, the main points in the article. Then add a final statement that summarizes any conclusions the author made in the article. Use the answers to the questions to help you.

   _____

   _____

   _____

   _____

   _____

   _____

   _____

   _____

A Does your paragraph answer all of the questions in Exercise B? Exchange papers with a partner and edit each other's papers. Use the Revising Checklist on page 77 to help you. Did you both include the same information? If not, what are the differences?

B Make sure the subjects and verbs in each sentence agree. Copy your revised summary on a separate piece of paper.

Paragraph Practice 3

Prewriting

A Read the article twice. Underline the main points during the second reading.

HURRICANE STRIKES—MANY HURT

Hurricane Irene hit southeastern Florida on Friday night, causing damage and destruction everywhere. The storm dumped 18 inches of rain on the area. The high winds that blew up to 85 miles per hour were responsible for most of the damage to the area. The winds knocked down trees and power lines, broke hotel windows, and damaged roofs. The wind also was to blame for ten serious injuries and several car accidents.

Much of the city was without electricity and water. In fact, hundreds of thousands of people had no electricity.

The hurricane caused severe flooding. Hundreds of people lost their homes or offices because of high winds and heavy rains. Some of the worst flooding was in Miami, where police sometimes needed boats to get through up to 4 feet of standing water. Thousands of acres of crops were

damaged or destroyed in South Florida, which supplies 75 percent of the nation's winter produce. "No one knows yet exactly how much money was lost in crop damage. I could not give you an estimate of damage to the crops, but I would not be surprised if it were $100 million," said the mayor of Miami.

Local officials called Irene the worst storm of the hurricane season for the area. It will take the people of Florida a long time to recover from the effects of this hurricane.

B Make a list of the important facts in the article. Try to include answers to the questions *Who?*, *What?*, *When?*, *Where?*, *Why?*, and *How?* on your list.

_____

_____

_____

_____

_____

_____

_____

 **C** Study your list. Make sure you have included only the main ideas. Cross out any details.

 Writing

Write a short, one-paragraph summary of the article. Make sure the subjects and verbs agree with each other.

_____

_____

_____

_____

_____

_____

 Revising

Compare your summary with some of your classmates' summaries. Have you included too much information? Did you miss an important idea? Do you need to cross out your own ideas? Revise your summary and then copy the final draft on a separate piece of paper.

Paragraph Practice 4

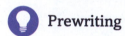 Prewriting

A Read the story and discuss it with a partner.

The Great Minu

Long ago, there was a poor man from a small town in the hills of Africa. His name was Younde. He was a simple farmer who had never been far from home. One day, he had to travel from his own little village to Accra, a big city near the ocean. He had heard about Accra and all the wonderful things there, but he had never seen it. He walked for many days. The road was hot and dusty. When he came close to Accra, he saw a little boy with a great herd of cows. He wondered who owned them. Younde asked the little boy, "Who is the owner of all these cows?" But the boy didn't understand Younde. Why? Younde's language was Akim, but the boy spoke Ga, the language of Accra. Finally the little boy said "Minu," which means "I don't understand" in the Ga language. But Younde thought that "Minu" was the name of the owner of the cows, so he exclaimed, "Mr. Minu must be very rich to own so many cows."

Then Younde entered the town. He saw women selling beautiful and extravagant things at the market. "Where do all these things come from?" he asked a woman. She smiled and said, "Minu." Younde was surprised. Again he said, "Mr. Minu must be very rich to own so many beautiful things."

After that, Younde saw a fine large building surrounded by beautiful gardens. Of course, he wondered who owned it. But once again, the man he asked could not understand Younde's question, so he also answered, "Minu." Younde couldn't believe his ears. "What a rich man Mr. Minu must be! He lives in such a huge and beautiful house!" cried Younde.

Next, Younde came to the beach. There he saw many fishing boats. Younde asked a fisherman, "Who owns all these boats?" "Minu," replied the fisherman. Again Younde misunderstood the answer. "These boats belong to the Great Minu also! He is the richest man I have ever heard of!" cried Younde. He was very impressed with everything he saw in Accra.

Finally, Younde started to walk home. As he passed down one of the streets of the town he saw a funeral procession. Several men were carrying a coffin. Many people, all dressed in black, were walking behind the coffin. Younde asked one of the mourners[1] who had died. The mourner sadly replied, "Minu." "Poor Mr. Minu!" cried Younde. "The Great Minu is dead. He has died just like an ordinary person!"

"Poor Minu!" he said over and over again. Younde continued on his way out of the city, but he couldn't get the tragedy of Minu from his mind. "Poor Minu! So he has had to leave all his wealth and beautiful things and die just as a poor person would do! Well, well—in the future I will be content with my small house and little money." And Younde went home quite pleased, back to his own little town.

[1] mourners: people who attend a funeral

B   With a partner. Make a list of the important facts in the story. Try to include facts about *Who?*, *What?*, *When?*, *Where?*, *Why?*, and *How?* on your list.

C   Study your list. Make sure you have included only the main ideas. Cross out any details.

Writing

On a separate piece of paper, write a one-paragraph summary of the story.

 **Revising**

A **Compare your summary with some of your classmates' summaries. As you are revising, think about these questions.**

1. Did you include too much information?

2. Did you miss an important idea?

3. Did you answer the questions *who, what, when, where, why,* and *how* in your summary?

B **Make sure the subjects and verbs agree with each other. Copy your revised summary on a separate piece of paper.**

ANSWERING TEST QUESTIONS

Teachers and professors often ask you to answer questions in paragraph form on tests or assignments.

> **WRITER'S TIP:** Answering Test Questions
>
> There are several helpful strategies to remember when writing paragraphs for tests.
>
> - Read the entire question carefully. Underline key words in the question.
> - Make sure you understand exactly what information you are being asked to write about (reasons, definitions, similarities, etc.).
> - Plan your answer.
> - Budget your time.

One way to begin writing your answer to a test question is to change the question into a statement. Use this statement as your topic sentence. Notice that sometimes the "question" is not written in question form, but in the imperative form. Study the examples.

Question: ***Why*** *are giant pandas in the wild threatened with extinction?*

Question: ***Explain why*** *giant pandas in the wild are threatened with extinction.*

Topic sentence: *There are several reasons why giant pandas in the wild are threatened with extinction.*

PRACTICE **A** **Change the following test questions into topic sentences.**

1. **Question:** Why is unemployment rising?

   _____

   _____

2. **Question:** What are the effects of radiation on the human body?

   _____

   _____

3. **Question:** Explain the reasons ice hockey is a dangerous sport.

_____

_____

4. **Question:** Explain the importance of Abraham Lincoln in American history.

_____

_____

5. **Question:** What were the causes of the Great Depression?

_____

_____

6. **Question:** How can genetically modified plants help solve the food shortage problem?

_____

_____

7. **Question:** What are the advantages and disadvantages of solar energy?

_____

_____

8. **Question:** Describe the four kinds of clouds.

_____

_____

9. **Question:** Describe the four stages involved in cell division.

_____

_____

B **Read the test question and student answer. Then discuss the questions that follow in groups.**

Question: Describe the three branches of government in the United States.

Answer: The United States' government has three main branches. The first branch is the legislative branch, which is called the Congress. Congress makes our laws. It is divided into two parts: the Senate and the House of Representatives. The Senate has 100 members, two from each state, who are elected for 6-year terms. The House of Representatives is made up of 435 members who are elected for 2-year terms. The number of representatives each state has is determined by its population. The second branch is the executive branch. The job of this branch is to ensure that the laws of the United States are obeyed. The President of the United

States is the head of the executive branch. The president also directs national defense and foreign policy. This branch is very big and includes the Vice President, department heads (Cabinet members), and heads of other agencies. Finally, the third branch is the judicial branch, which is headed by the Supreme Court. It oversees the court system of the United States. Its powers include interpreting the Constitution, and reviewing laws. It also settles disagreements between individuals and the government.

1. Does the topic sentence restate the question?

   _____

2. Does the answer describe each branch of government?

   _____

3. Underline the signal words the student used.

4. What specific information (details such as numbers and times) did the student include?

   _____

   _____

   _____

Writing Responses to Test Questions

  Imagine that you have studied the information in the boxes in class. You are expected to learn and to remember the information, and use it to answer questions on the test. Read the information and discuss it with a partner to make sure you understand it.

The Eye

The human eye has an iris that gets bigger or smaller to let in the right amount of light. It also has a lens that focuses the light into a clear picture. In the eye, light forms a picture on the retina. The nerve cells in the retina send a picture message to the brain. The picture the brain receives is upside down. The brain then interprets the message so that what you see is right side up.

The Camera

The camera has a diaphragm that gets bigger or smaller to let in the right amount of light. It also has a lens that focuses the light into a clear picture. In a camera, light forms a picture on film. The picture is upside down on the film.

B   **Use the information you remember from exercise A to answer the following test question.**

Question: Discuss the similarities between the eye and the camera.

_____

_____

_____

_____

_____

_____

_____

_____

_____

_____

YOU BE THE EDITOR

Read the paragraph. It contains nine mistakes. Correct the mistakes. Copy the answer on a separate piece of paper.

Languages change and evolve over time, much in the same way as cultures changes. One way languages change are by adding new words. This often happens through contact and interaction with another language, often through travel and trade. Results in the borrowing of words. For example, when people from different places trades with each other. They pick up specific words and phrases for trade objects. languages also change as they develop new words for new technologies and ideas. For instance, the words _retweet, staycation, emoji,_ and _meme_ have all been added to official english dictionaries in the past a few years.

ON YOUR OWN

Find an article on the Internet or in a book, magazine, or newspaper. Read it carefully and write a one-paragraph summary of it. Bring the article and your summary to class. Exchange summaries with a classmate and give each other suggestions for improving the summary.

In this chapter, you will practice writing personal and business letters.

"Okay, mom...my letter is all written and sealed...where's the 'send' button?"

PERSONAL LETTERS

Personal letters are letters to a friend or relative. They include information about yourself, and ask questions about your friends and relatives. Personal letters are informal and are often handwritten. There are five main parts to a personal letter.

Date ——————[September 8, 2017

Dear Cassie,]—————— Greeting

Thanks for the wonderful week I spent with you and your family. Your
mother is such a terrific cook! I think I must have gained 10 pounds in just
the 7 days I was there. It was really nice of you to take the week off to
spend time with me and show me so many places. I really enjoyed meeting
your friends. I hope you'll be able to visit my part of the country soon.
Thanks again for a wonderful time. Keep in touch.   — Message

Best,]—————— Closing

Candace]—————— Signature

WRITER'S TIP: Personal Letters

Remember these guidelines when you write a personal letter.

- The date goes in the upper right corner.

- The most common greeting is *Dear.* Other informal greetings include *Hi* and *Hello.*

- You can use contractions: ***I'll** text you soon.*

- You can use idioms: *Remember, this is a secret. Please don't **spill the beans.***

- You can use abbreviations: *I hope to see you by the end of **Feb.***

- You can ask personal questions: ***How's your new roommate?***

Candace Graham
327 South 2nd Street
Philadelphia, PA 19012

Return Adrees
(your address)

Ms. Cassie Lourie
52 Main Street
Conby, OR 99106

Addressee
(person receiving letter)

WRITER'S TIP: Addressing Envelopes

Use the following form for the envelope of a personal letter.

- The return address of the person who writes the letter goes in the upper left-hand corner.

- The address of the person who will receive the letter goes in the center of the envelope.

- The stamp goes in the upper right-hand corner.

WRITING PERSONAL LETTERS

Personal Letter 1

Write a personal letter to a friend you haven't seen recently. Tell your friend what is new in your life. Also, ask some questions about his or her life.

_____

_____

_____

_____

_____

_____

_____

_____

_____

_____

_____

Personal Letter 2

A Write a short letter to each of the following people. Write each on a separate piece of paper. Bring to class a properly addressed envelope for each letter.

1. Invite your friend to come visit you.

2. Thank your relative for a gift he or she sent you.

3. Tell your parents about an important decision you made.

B Exchange letters with a partner. Read your partner's letter. Pretend you are the person receiving the letter and write a response to each one.

BUSINESS LETTERS

Business letters are more formal than personal letters. They are usually written to someone you do not know. You might write a business letter to request information or to inform someone about a problem. Look at the model business letter. There are six parts to a business letter. There are several acceptable formats you can use for a business letter, but the block format shown here is the easiest and most common. In the block format, all parts of the letter begin on the left margin.

177 Atlantic Avenue
Boston, Massachusetts 02140
April 22, 2010

Heading (your address and date)

Director of Admissions
University of Michigan
1220 Student Activities Building
515 E. Jefferson
Ann Arbor, MI 48109-1316

**Inside Address
(name or position and address
of person receiving letter**

Dear Sir or Madam:

Greeting

I am a senior at Springfield Academy, and I am interested
in attending The University of Michigan to study
engineering. Please send me the appropriate application
forms and any information you have about the
undergraduate engineering program. I will also need
information about TOEFL requirements because English
is not my native language.

Message

I look forward to hearing from you.

Sincerely,

Closing

Hasan Halkali

Hasan Halkali

Signature

WRITER'S TIP: Business Letters

Remember these guidelines for writing business letters.

- Business letters in English almost always begin with **Dear** . . . even if you do not know the person. Look at the examples.

  Dear Mr. Becker: *Dear Mrs. Becker:*   *Dear Ms. Becker:*   *Dear Dr. Lim:*
  Dear Sir: *Dear Madam:*   *Dear Sir or Madam:*

- Identify yourself and state the purpose of your letter at the beginning. Go directly to the point. Be brief and clear.

- Type business letters if possible.

- Do not write about personal topics.

- Do not ask personal information (age, health, family) of the person you are writing to.

- Do not use slang, informal phrases, or contractions.

- Business letters end with a formal closing. The most common closing is *Sincerely*. Other formal closings include **Kind regards**, **Yours truly**, **Best wishes**.

GRAMMAR FOR WRITING: Capitalization and Punctuation in Letters

English has certain rules for capitalization and punctuation in letter writing. Learning these rules will improve your letters.

Study the rules.

Rule	Examples
Capitalize the first word in the greeting. Capitalize all nouns or titles in the greeting	**D**ear **P**enny, **D**ear **U**ncle **T**om, **D**ear **C**oach **B**aker: **D**ear **D**r. **B**ruce:
Capitalize the first word in the closing.	**Y**ours truly, **K**ind regards, **B**est wishes,
Capitalize the name of your street, city, state, and country.	21 **W**ilson **R**oad **F**ayetteville, **NY**
Capitalize the name of months.	**M**arch **D**ecember
Capitalize the names of people (first and last names).	**F**aruk **L**arry **P**almer
Capitalize the pronoun *I*.	Harry and **I** look forward to seeing you soon.
Capitalize the first letter of every new sentence.	**P**lease send me information about registering for the conference.
Use a comma after the greeting in friendly letters.	Dear Joan**,**
Use a comma between city and state.	Syracuse**,** NY
Use a comma in the date between the day and the year.	June 28**,** 2015
Use a comma after the closing.	Love, Best wishes, Sincerely yours,
Use a colon in the greeting after the name in business letters.	Dear Ms. Dalton: Dear Professor Berger:
Use correct end punctuation at the end of every sentence.	Please send me the necessary forms. Thank you for your quick response.

A **Circle the twenty mistakes in capitalization and punctuation in this friendly letter.**

april 7. 2016

dear pamela

thanks so much for your letter. It sounds like you are very busy this semester. i am, too. Business school is getting harder. i'm taking economics and statistics, and both courses are difficult. luckily, my roommate, evelyn, is majoring in economics, so she can help me. I like living in the dorm, and it's really easy to make friends here. Unfortunately, it's often noisy and hard to study in my room. I'm planning to get my own apartment next year.

I'm coming to dallas next weekend to visit my cousins. I hope we can get together. Are you free on saturday evening Maybe we can meet for dinner. My aunt paula is going to make reservations for 7:30 at maxwell's. It's a new restaurant, and it's gotten great reviews. I hope you can meet us I'll call you next week to make plans.

love

cathy

B **Circle the twenty-seven mistakes in capitalization and punctuation in this business letter.**

240 broad street
newtown. iowa 50208
may 17. 2016
gail stevens, Housing Director

english language Program
345 howard Avenue
Madison. wisconsin 10002

dear ms. stevens,

i am writing for information about housing for the fall semester of 2016. I am preregistered as a full-time student in your English Language Program. please let me know if dormitories are available for international students. If that is not a possibility, i would like to live with a host family. I am from japan, so living with an american family would help my english. Please send me the necessary information and any forms that I need to submit.

I look forward to hearing from you.

Sincerely:

sakura hayashi

Identifying Formal and Informal Phrases

Most English words are both formal and informal. However, some English words and phrases are considered informal and are only used in informal writing situations. Other words and phrases are usually used in formal writing, such as academic writing and business writing. Many dictionaries will tell you if a word or phrase is informal.

PRACTICE **In each of the following pairs, one sentence or phrase is appropriate for formal letters, but the other one should be used only in informal letters. Write _F_ for formal and _I_ for informal.**

1. _____ I'm really sorry about what happened.

   _____ I would like to apologize for the inconvenience this caused you.

2. _____ I look forward to hearing from you soon.

   _____ I can't wait to hear from you.

3. _____ Dear Julie,

   _____ Dear Mrs. Brody:

4. _____ Yours truly,

   _____ Love,

5. _____ I will call you Monday morning.

   _____ I'll give you a call on Mon.

6. _____ I appreciate your help in this matter.

   _____ Thanks a lot for helping me.

7. _____ To ask for more info, call my assistant.

   _____ To request additional information, please contact the admissions office.

WRITING BUSINESS LETTERS

Business Letter 1

A Read the advertisement for the Philadelphia Orchestra.

B Write a letter requesting tickets. In your letter you will need to state the following:

- the date and time of the performance you want to attend
- the number and price of the tickets you want
- whether you are including your credit card number or a check

_____

_____

_____

_____

_____

_____

_____

_____

_____

_____

_____

_____

_____

C Read your letter again. Use the Business Letter Revising Checklist and make corrections if necessary.

BUSINESS LETTER REVISING CHECKLIST		
	YES	NO
1. Have you included both a heading and an inside address?		
2. Is there a colon after the greeting?		
3. Is the letter direct and to the point?		
4. Is there a comma after the closing?		
5. Have you signed the letter?		
6. Is the punctuation, spelling, and grammar correct?		

D Copy it on a separate piece of paper.

Business Letter 2

A Choose one of the following tasks. Make a list of ideas you want to include in your letter.
- Write to a college admissions office asking for information.
- Write to a radio station requesting more information about a product you heard advertised.
- Write a letter to a company stating that you ordered a product three months ago but haven't received it yet.
- Write a letter of importance to you.

_____   _____

_____   _____

_____   _____

_____   _____

B Write your letter on a separate piece of paper.

C Revise your letter. Use the Business Letter Revising Checklist above to help you. Make corrections if necessary.

D Bring your finished letter to class in a properly addressed envelope. Use the same format for a business letter envelope that you use for a personal letter envelope. Exchange letters with a classmate and give each other suggestions for improving your letters.

LETTERS OF COMPLAINT AND PRAISE

 A **Read the following business letter of complaint and answer the questions.**

1123 Gardner Street
Swansea, Massachusetts 02777

April 17, 2016

Ms. Samantha Stiller, Customer Service Manager
Beauty Glow Cosmetics Company
234 Philip Place
Oswego, NY 13126

Dear Ms. Stiller:

I have been using Beauty Glow products for many years, and I have always been very pleased with them. However, last week I bought a bottle of your newest perfume, Rose Petal, and I was very disappointed. First of all, the perfume stained my blouse. It also caused my skin to itch and burn. Finally, the sprayer broke the first time I used it. I feel that this product does not meet your standards of high quality. I am enclosing my receipt from the store. Please send me a refund. I look forward to hearing from you soon.

Sincerely,

Charlotte Sherden

Charlotte Sherden

1. What is Charlotte complaining about?

_____

2. Why was she unsatisfied with the product? What three reasons does she mention?

_____

_____

_____

3. What does Charlotte want the company to do?

_____

B Read the model business letter of praise and discuss it with a partner. Underline words and expressions the writer used to show that he was satisfied.

123 Main Street
Marlton, MA 02777

March 12, 2016

Mr. Barry Douglas, Store Manager
The Computer World
45 Side Street
Marlton, MA 02778

Dear Mr. Douglas:

I am writing to let you know that I appreciate the excellent customer service your employees gave me last week. I went to your store to buy a new laptop. Everyone on your staff was very helpful. The salespeople I worked with, especially Lucy White and Michael Caldwell, were very knowledgeable about laptop computers. They helped me choose the laptop that best met my needs. They also advised me about what kind of laptop case I should buy.

My new laptop works very well and it is quite fast. I am very satisfied with my purchase, and I will go back to your store for all my computer needs. Please thank Lucy and Michael for me.

Sincerely,

Ian Parker

Ian Parker

Letter 1

 A Read the situation and discuss it with a partner.

Situation: Two weeks ago you called the person who lives above you in your apartment building. You were upset because he was playing his stereo so loudly. In fact, he often plays it very loudly all day long, so it bothers you when you are trying to study. He also plays it late at night when you are trying to sleep. When you spoke with him on the phone, he said that he would try to keep the volume lower. The first few days it was better, but now it is a problem again. You are trying to study for your final exams. It is very difficult because of the constant noise.

B Write a polite note to your neighbor asking him to be more considerate.

_____

_____

_____

_____

_____

_____

C It is now one week later and the noise has gotten even worse. You are furious. Write an angry letter to your landlord, Lorna Taylor, threatening to break your lease and move out if she does not do something about the noise.

_____

_____

_____

_____

_____

_____

_____

_____

_____

_____

_____

_____

_____

_____

Letter 2

(A) **Discuss the following topics in a small group.**

- a great experience you had at a hotel or restaurant
- a bad experience you had at a hotel or restaurant

(B) **Write a business letter to the manager of the hotel or restaurant. Describe the great or bad experience you had.**

_____

_____

_____

_____

_____

_____

_____

_____

_____

_____

_____

_____

_____

_____

_____

(C) **Exchange letters with a partner. Give each other suggestions for improving your letters. Revise your letter. You can also use the Business Letter Revising Checklist on page 236 to help you.**

(D) **Copy your revised letter on a separate piece of paper.**

YOU BE THE EDITOR

Read the personal letter. It contains nine mistakes. Correct the mistakes. Copy the corrected letter on a separate piece of paper.

June 22, 2016

dear Ben:

    I just visited the Morgan Motor Company factory in malvern, England, I felt like I was back in the 1920s. There are computers and other modern equipment, but I soon realized that most things have not changed. Morgans is still made the old-fashioned way. Each one is built by hand no two are exactly alike. Only about ten cars are made per week. That's why there is a five-year waiting list for a new one. Morgans don't have power steering, power brakes, or radios. But, they do have a loyal fan club. Morgan lovers can talk for hours about the thrill of feeling every bump in the road, of listening to the roar of the wind, and of smelling the sweet perfume of burning oil as you drive. I'm enclosing a picture I took of one of the Morgans. I put my name on the waiting list for a new Morgan!

Love,

jackson

ON YOUR OWN

Write a letter to a friend or relative who has moved or is far away. Describe what has happened in your life since you last saw the person. Exchange your letter with a classmate and give each other suggestions for improving your letters. Then address an envelope and mail the letter.

You Be the Editor: Answer Key

Chapter 1, page 9

A Smart Man

Many of the stories in my country, ~~turkey~~ *Turkey*, are about a clever man named ~~nasreddin~~ *Nasreddin*. In one story, ~~nasreddin~~ *Nasreddin* is walking through the marketplace when an angry shopkeeper stops him *.* The shopkeeper yells at ~~nasreddin~~ *Nasreddin* for not paying the seventy-five piasters he owes him. But the clever Nasreddin says, "~~you~~ *You* know that ~~i~~ *I* plan to pay you thirty-five piasters tomorrow, and next ~~tuesday~~ *Tuesday* another thirty-five. ~~that~~ *That* means ~~i~~ *I* owe you only five piasters. You should be ashamed for yelling at me so loudly for a debt of only five piasters!" I laugh every time I think of that story.

Chapter 2, page 31

Erik's Favorite Sports

Erik ~~enjoy~~ *enjoys* many types of sports. He ~~is liking~~ *likes* team sports such as basketball, soccer, and baseball. In fact, he is the ~~Captain~~ *captain* of the basketball team at our school. ~~erik~~ *Erik* also plays individual sports like squash, tennis, and golf very ~~good~~ *well*. Last year, he ~~win~~ *won* two golf tournaments and most of the tennis matches he played. His ~~favorites~~ *favorite* sports involve ~~dangerous~~ *danger* as well as excitement. He is ~~no~~ *not* afraid to go extreme skiing or skydiving. He is an excellent athlete ~~,~~ *. It* ~~it~~ was not a surprise when Erik won the sports award at graduation.

Chapter 3, page 46

Mathematics throughout ~~history~~ *History*

Throughout history, people have done mathematical computations and kept accounts. ~~in~~ *In*
early ~~Times~~ *times*, people used groups of sticks or stones to help make calculations. Then the abacus
was developed in ~~china~~ *China*. This simple method represents the beginnings of data processing~~?~~ *.* As
computational needs became more complicated, people developed more advanced technologies.
~~On~~ *In* 1642, Blaise ~~pascal~~ *Pascal* developed the first simple adding machine in ~~france~~ *France*. Later, in England in
1830, ~~charles~~ *Charles* Babbage designed the first machine that did calculations and printed out results.
Finally, ~~In~~ *in* the middle of the twentieth century, researchers at the University of ~~pennsylvania~~ *Pennsylvania* built the
first electronic computer. Today, of course, we have the computer to perform all kinds of advanced
mathematical computations.

Chapter 4, page 61

The Many Uses of Corn

There are several reasons why corn is one of the most important food sources in the world~~, it~~ *. It*
has many other important ~~use~~ *uses* as well. First of all, one of the most ~~valuables~~ *valuable* uses of corn is as an
alternative energy source. Ethanol, which is ~~make~~ *made* from corn, is used to fuel cars and planes. ~~some~~ *Some*
houses are even heated with ethanol fuel. Corn is also used to make plastics and fabrics. In fact, corn
~~are~~ *is* used in thousands of products such as glue, shoe polish, aspirin, ink, and cosmetics. Finally, the
syrup from corn sweetens ~~Ice~~ *ice* cream, soda, and candy. Scientists continue to ~~researches~~ *research* new uses of
corn~~, they~~ *. They* find more every year.

Chapter 5, page 71

My Bright, Sunny Kitchen

I love to spend time *a* my kitchen. It is big, sunny room with white walls and a grey tile floor. When

you enter the kitchen, there is a small desk to the left. Above the desk, I have a bookshelf with my

cookbooks. The dishwasher is next to the desk *on* of the right. The refrigerator and oven are along the

back wall, *and* so there is a long grey and white marble counter between them. The microwave is at one

end of that counter, and the toaster oven and coffee maker are at the other end. *The* the sink is in the

middle of the counter. There is a window above the sink, and lots of cabinets on each side of the

window and below the sink. In the middle of the room, *I* i have a round table with four *chairs* chair. I have a

vase with flowers *in* at the middle of the table. On the wall *to* in the left of the door is a pantry with food

and spices.

Chapter 6, page 86

How to *Improve* improve Your Performance on an Exam

There are several *things* thing you can do to improve your performance on an exam. First, *you* should get

a good night's sleep the night before the test. *That* that means sleeping for at least eight *hours* hour. It is also

important to eat a good breakfast on the morning of the exam, *so* you won't *be* have hungry during the

exam. Finally, to bring a bottle of water to the test in case you *get* got thirsty. Just don't drink too much, or

you may have to get up in the middle of the exam for a bathroom break.

Chapter 7, page 86

Skyscrapers on the Rise

Skyscrapers are on the rise. A building called Burj Khalifa ~~on~~ *in* the United Arab Emirates city of ~~dubai~~ *Dubai* is 2,722 ~~feets~~ *feet* tall. That makes it the tallest building in the world. Until recently, the world's tallest building was in Taipei, Taiwan. ~~this~~ *This* office building in the heart of the busy capital city ~~have~~ *has* 101 floors, which is where it gets its name, Taipei 101. Recently, however, engineers and architects in Saudi Arabia began work on a new skyscraper that will surpass both Taipei 101 and Burj Khalifa in height. It *will be* ^ 1 kilometer tall. The Kingdom Tower, as it is being called, will be twice as tall as the Burj Khalifa. Adrian Smith, the chief architect says, "~~the~~ *The* tower will represent the new spirit in Saudi Arabia, which symbolizes the Kingdom as an important global business and cultural leader, and demonstrates the strength and creative vision of its people." With so many tall buildings all over the world, ~~Tourists~~ *tourists* will have to get used to looking up more often.

Chapter 8, page 126

How to Remove the Shell ~~From~~ *from* a Lobster

It is not difficult to remove the shell from a lobster if you follow these ~~step~~ *steps*. First, ~~to~~ put the lobster on ~~it's~~ *its* back and remove the two large claws and tail section. After that, ~~You~~ *you* must also twist off the flippers at end of the tail section. After these are twisted off, use ~~you~~ *your* fingers to push the lobster meat out of the tail in one piece. Next, ~~removing~~ *remove* the black vein *vein from* ~~From~~ the tail meat. Finally, before you sit down to enjoy your meal, break open the claws with a nutcracker and remove the meat.

Chapter 9, page 146

Dog Missing

My adorable dog, Bette, is missing. She is a ~~small~~ black *small* poodle with ~~browns~~ *brown* eyes. She has ~~hair~~ *hair.* short curly. Bette weighs 8 pounds and is about one and a half feet long. She has a ~~tail~~ short, long *tail* floppy ears, and small feet. She is ~~wear~~ *wearing* a silver collar with an ID tag on it. She is very friendly around people, *and* she loves children. I have had Bette since she was a puppy *and* I miss her very much. I am offering a $50 reward for anyone who finds Bette. Please ~~calling~~ *call* or text me at 305-892-7671.

Chapter 10, page 166

Suleiman the Magnificent

In ~~me~~ *my* opinion, Suleiman was one of the greatest leaders of all time *. He* ~~he~~ accomplished more than any other ruler of the Ottoman Empire. During his reign ~~at~~ *from* 1520 to 1566, Suleiman ~~expanding~~ *expanded* the size of the Ottoman Empire to include parts of Asia, ~~europe~~ *Europe*, and Africa. While Suleiman's military victories made him a well-respected world leader *, he* ~~He~~ did many other important things for the empire as well. For example *,* Suleiman introduced a new system of law. ~~he~~ *He* also promoted education, architecture, and the arts. Therefore, I ~~belief~~ *believe* he deserves the name "Suleiman the Magnificent."

Chapter 11, page 191

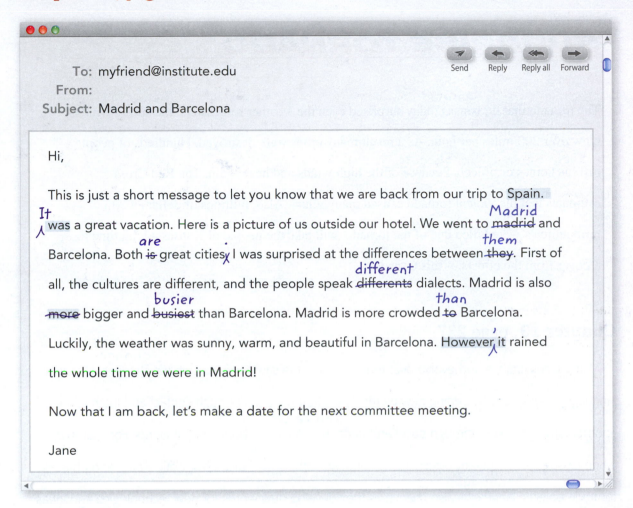

To: myfriend@institute.edu

From:

Subject: Madrid and Barcelona

Hi,

This is just a short message to let you know that we are back from our trip to Spain. It was a great vacation. Here is a picture of us outside our hotel. We went to ~~madrid~~ Madrid and Barcelona. Both ~~is~~ are great cities. I was surprised at the differences between ~~they~~ them. First of all, the cultures are different, and the people speak ~~differents~~ different dialects. Madrid is also ~~more~~ bigger and ~~busiest~~ busier than Barcelona. Madrid is more crowded ~~to~~ than Barcelona.

Luckily, the weather was sunny, warm, and beautiful in Barcelona. However, it rained the whole time we were in Madrid!

Now that I am back, let's make a date for the next committee meeting.

Jane

Chapter 12, page 212

SURPRISE TORNADO

August 3.

The tornado that hit ~~kansas~~ *Kansas* today surprised even the weather forecasters. ~~the~~ *The* strong winds

blew over 200 miles per hour. As a result, many crops were destroyed. Hundreds of people

lost ~~his~~ *their* homes or offices, ~~Because~~ *because* of the high winds and heavy rain. The Red Cross

estimates that the violent tornado caused many ~~injury~~ *injuries*. Also, millions of dollars worth of

farm animals were killed due ~~of~~ *to* the tornado. *It* will take the people of Kansas a long time to

recover from the effects of this tornado.

Chapter 13, page 227

   Languages change and evolve over time, much in the same way as cultures ~~changes~~ *change*. One way

languages change ~~are~~ *is* by adding new words. This often happens through contact and interaction with

another language, often through travel and trade. ~~Results~~ *This results* in the borrowing of words. For example,

when people from different places ~~trades~~ *trade* with each other, ~~They~~ *they* pick up specific words and phrases

for trade objects. ~~languages~~ *Languages* also change as they develop new words for new technologies and ideas.

For instance, the words *retweet*, *staycation*, *emoji*, and *meme* ~~has~~ *have* all been added to official ~~english~~ *English*

dictionaries in the past a few years.

June 22, 2016

Dear ,
~~dear~~ Ben X

    I just visited the Morgan Motor Company factory in ~~malvern~~ Malvern,
England, and I felt like I was back in the 1920s. There ~~are~~ were computers and other
modern equipment, but I soon realized that most things have not changed.
Morgans ~~is~~ are still made the old-fashioned way. Each one is built by hand, so no
two are exactly alike. Only about ten cars are made per week. That's why
there is a five-year waiting list for a new one. Morgans don't have power
steering, power brakes, or radios. But, they do have a loyal fan club. Morgan
lovers can talk for hours about the thrill of feeling every bump in the road,
of listening to the roar of the wind, and of smelling the sweet perfume of
burning oil as you drive. I'm enclosing a picture I took of one of the Morgans.
I put my name ~~in~~ on the waiting list for a new Morgan!

Love,

Jackson
~~jackson~~

Appendix

Spelling Rules

Simple Present Singular Verbs with *He*, *She*, and *It*

1. For most verbs, add the letter "s" to the base form of the verb
   Examples: *play – plays   walk – walks   write – writes*

2. For verbs that end in "-sh", "-ch", "-ss", "x", add "-es"
   Examples: *rush – rushes   watch – watches   miss – misses   box – boxes*

3. For verbs that end in a consonant + "y", change "y" to "i" and then add "-es"
   Examples: *fly – flies   try – tries   carry – carries*

Adding *-ing*

1. For most verbs, add "-ing" to the base form of the verb
   Examples: *play – playing   jump – jumping   go – going*

2. For verbs that end in "e", drop the final "-e" and add "-ing"
   Examples: *leave – leaving   make – making   receive – receiving*

3. For most verbs that end in consonant-vowel-consonant (CVC) combination, double the last consonant and then add "-ing"
   Examples: *sit – sitting   run – running   begin – beginning*

4. For verbs that end in "ie", change the "ie" to "y" then add "-ing"
   Examples: *die – dying   lie – lying*

Exceptions:

1. Do <u>not</u> double the last consonant in verbs that end in "w", "x", or "y"
   Examples: *sew – sewing   fix – fixing   enjoy – enjoying*

2. Do <u>not</u> double the last consonant if the last syllable of a verb is not stressed
   Examples: *happen – happening   listen – listening*

Simple Past of Regular Verbs

1. For most verbs, add "-ed" to the base form of the verb
   Examples: *play – played   jump – jumped*

2. For verbs that end in "e," add "-d" to the end.
   Examples: *hope – hoped   love – loved   save – saved*

3. For most verbs that end in consonant-vowel-consonant (CVC) combination, double the last consonant and then add "-ed"
   Examples: *stop – stopped   plan – planned   beg – begged*

4. For verbs that end in consonant + "y", drop the "y" and add "-ied"
   Examples: *study – studied   hurry – hurried   try – tried*

Exceptions:

1. Do <u>not</u> double the last consonant in verbs that end in "w", "x", or "y"
   Examples: sew – sewed   fix – fixed   enjoy – enjoyed

2. Do <u>not</u> double the last consonant if the last syllable of a verb is not stressed
   Examples: happen – happened   listen – listened

Irregular Verbs

Here are a few simple rules to help you find the correct ending for different verbs:

A. **Verbs which end in a consonant and a silent "e"**, such as *like, hope, create, advise, amuse*

   1. In the **present** tense, you add "**s**" to the **he**, **she**, or **it** forms:
      She **likes** cheese.
      He **loves** her.

   2. In the **past** tense, you add "**d**" to all forms:
      She **created** a terrible noise.
      They **liked** the movie.
      He **hoped** to win a prize.

   3. In the **continuous** tenses, you take away the "**e**" and add "**ing**."
      She's **hoping** to pass the test.
      I was just **admiring** your new car.

B. **Verbs which end in "y"** (NOT verbs which end in *-ay, -oy, -uy, -ey*)

   1. In the **present** or **past** tenses, you change "**y**" into "**ie**."
      cry   — The baby **cries** a lot.
              She **cried** all night.
      worry — It **worries** me.
              He **worried** his mother.

   2. In the **continuous** tenses, you do not change the "**y**". You add "**ing**" to the "**y**."
      dry   — She's **drying** her hair.
      hurry — He's **hurrying** to work.
      fry   — She's **frying** an egg.

C. **Verbs which double the consonant**

   1. If a verb has one syllable and ends in a single vowel and a consonant, such as **hit**, **clap**, **plan**, **pin**, the consonant is usually doubled:
      clap   — She **clapped** her hands.
      plan   — I'm **planning** to go home tomorrow.

   2. If a verb has more than one syllable, but ends in a single vowel and a consonant, and has the stress on the last syllable, the consonant is usually doubled:
      begin — I'm **beginning** to understand.
      upset — She's really **upsetting** me.

   3. If a verb has more than one syllable and the stress is **not** on the last syllable, the last consonant is not usually doubled:
      offer   — She **offered** me some coffee.
      open   — He **opened** the door.

4. If the last vowel sound of a verb is written with two letters, you do **not** double the final consonant:

heat — I'm **heating** the soup.
cook — He **cooked** our dinner.

Gerunds and Infinitives

Gerunds

A gerund is verb form that we use as a noun. We form gerunds by adding -ing to the base form of the verb, for example, *read – reading*. You can use a gerund as the subject, the complement, or the object of a sentence.

Examples:

Reading helps your vocabulary. (*Reading* is the subject of the sentence.)
My hobby is reading. (*Reading* is the complement of the sentence.)
She enjoys reading. (*Reading* is the object of the sentence.)

Infinitives

Infinitives are the form of the verb including "to," for example, *to read*. We usually use infinitives as the object of a sentence.

Example:

He wants to read. (*To read* is the object of the sentence.)

Both gerunds and infinitives can be used as the subject, but gerunds are much more common.

Examples:

More Common: *Reading is important.*
Less Common: *To read is important.*

Gerunds and infinitives can both be used as the object. The main verb in the sentence determines whether you use a gerund or an infinitive.

Examples:

He enjoys swimming. (*Enjoy* requires a gerund.)
He wants to swim. (*Want* requires an infinitive.)

These verbs can be followed by gerunds as objects.

avoid	I avoid driving in the snow.
enjoy	He enjoys flying.
finish	She finished writing her essay yesterday.
quit	I quit driving a taxi last month.
miss	I miss living in a warm climate.
practice	They practice speaking English as often as possible.

These verbs can be followed by infinitives as objects.

decide	She decided to take a vacation.
want	I want to learn Japanese.
hope	They hope to study abroad.
need	I need to clean my apartment.
plan	We plan to take an English course.
promise	I promise to drive you to the airport.

These verbs can be followed by gerunds or infinitives. The meaning is the same.

	Gerund	Infinitive
begin	I began learning Arabic as a young child.	I began to learn Arabic as a young child.
like	He likes swimming.	He likes to swim.
hate	She hates flying.	She hates to fly.
start	I started studying after dinner.	I started to study after dinner.
love	I love exercising.	I love to exercise.
prefer	We prefer eating at home.	We prefer to eat at home.

Common Noncount Nouns

Count nouns can be counted, but noncount nouns cannot be counted. Here is a chart of some common noncount nouns.

Category	Examples
Food	rice, sugar, salt, pepper, soup. beef, bread, butter, fish, meat
Liquids	coffee, gasoline, milk, oil, soup, syrup, tea, water, juice
Activities	homework, housework, music, reading, singing, sleeping, soccer, tennis, work
Groups of Similar Items	clothing, furniture, hardware, luggage, equipment, mail, money, software
Subjects	English, math, science. music, biology
Natural Events	electricity, gravity, heat, humidity, rain, snow, sunshine, thunder
Materials	aluminum, , chalk, cloth, concrete, cotton, glue, lumber, wood, wool, plastic
Abstract	advice, courage, enjoyment, fun, help, honesty, information, intelligence, knowledge, luck, patience

Common Abbreviations

People

Mr.   – Mister
Mrs.   – Mistress
Ms.
Dr.   – Doctor
Jr.   – Junior
Sr.   – Senior

Months of the Year

Jan.   – January
Feb.   – February
Mar.   – March
Apr.   – April
Aug.   – August
Sept. – September
Oct.   – October
Nov.   – November
Dec.   – December

Days of the Week

Mon.   – Monday
Tues. – Tuesday
Wed.   – Wednesday
Thurs. – Thursday
Fri.   – Friday
Sat.   – Saturday
Sun.   – Sunday

States of the United States

Perhaps the most commonly used abbreviations used in the U.S. are found in the names of the 50 states:

AL – Alabama	MT – Montana
AK – Alaska	NE – Nebraska
AZ – Arizona	NV – Nevada
AR – Arkansas	NH – New Hampshire
CA – California	NJ – New Jersey
CO – Colorado	NM – New Mexico
CT – Connecticut	NY – New York
DE – Delaware	NC – North Carolina
FL – Florida	ND – North Dakota
GA – Georgia	OH – Ohio
HI – Hawaii	OK – Oklahoma
ID – Idaho	OR – Oregon
IL – Illinois	PA – Pennsylvania
IN – Indiana	RI – Rhode Island
IA – Iowa	SC – South Carolina
KS – Kansas	SD – South Dakota
KY – Kentucky	TN – Tennessee
LA – Louisiana	TX – Texas
ME – Maine	UT – Utah
MD – Maryland	VT – Vermont
MA – Massachusetts	VA – Virginia
MI – Michigan	WA – Washington
MN – Minnesota	WV – West Virginia
MS – Mississippi	WI – Wisconsin
MO – Missouri	WY – Wyoming

Map of the United States and Canada

ATLANTIC OCEAN

Newfoundland
NOVA SCOTIA
PRINCE EDWARD ISLAND
NEW HAMPSHIRE
VERMONT
MASSACHUSETTS
RHODE ISLAND
CONNECTICUT
NEW JERSEY
DELAWARE
MARYLAND
Washington, DC
MAINE
Augusta
NEW BRUNSWICK
Boston
NEW YORK
New York
Philadelphia
PENNSYLVANIA
VIRGINIA
WEST VIRGINIA
NORTH CAROLINA
Charlotte
Charleston
SOUTH CAROLINA
Miami
FLORIDA
Tampa

Churchill Falls
Nain
Sept-Îles
Ungava Bay
QUEBEC
Québec
Kuujjuaq
Montreal
OTTAWA
Toronto
Cleveland
OHIO
Indianapolis
Louisville
KENTUCKY
TENNESSEE
Memphis
Appalachian Mountains
Atlanta
GEORGIA
ALABAMA

HUDSON BAY
ONTARIO
Detroit
MICHIGAN
INDIANA
Chicago
ILLINOIS
Milwaukee
WISCONSIN
Thunder Bay
St. Louis
MISSOURI
ARKANSAS
Little Rock
Jackson
MISSISSIPPI
LOUISIANA
Mississippi River

Sandy Lake
MANITOBA
MINNESOTA
Minneapolis
IOWA
Omaha
Kansas City
KANSAS
Oklahoma City
OKLAHOMA
Dallas
Houston
San Antonio
Austin
TEXAS
GULF OF MEXICO

NUNAVUT
Baker Lake (Qamanittuaq)
NORTH DAKOTA
Bismark
SOUTH DAKOTA
Pierre
NEBRASKA
Missouri River

SASKATCHEWAN
Saskatoon
Great Slave Lake
MONTANA
Helena
WYOMING
Cheyenne
Denver
COLORADO
Santa Fe
Albuquerque
NEW MEXICO
MEXICO
CANADA

ALBERTA
Calgary
Rocky Mountains
IDAHO
Boise
Salt Lake City
UTAH
NEVADA
Las Vegas
ARIZONA
Phoenix
Tucson

BRITISH COLUMBIA
Kamloops
Vancouver
Victoria
Seattle
WASHINGTON
Portland
OREGON
Sierra Nevada Mountains
CALIFORNIA
San Francisco
Los Angeles
San Diego

BERING SEA
ALASKA
PACIFIC OCEAN

Hawaii

Photo Credits

Page 1: Copyright 2004 by Randy Glasbergen/www.glasbergen.com; 10: Andy Dean Photography/Shutterstock; 32: © Randy Glasbergen/www.glasbergen.com; 41: Popova Olga/Fotolia; 42: Epa european pressphoto agency b.v./Alamy Stock Photo; 47: © Randy Glasbergen/www.glasbergen.com; 58: Pavel Ganchev Paf/Shutterstock; 72: Copyright 2005 by Randy Glasbergen/www.glasbergen.com; 89: Rozakov/Fotolia; 099 (bottom): 123RF; 99 (top): BioLife Pics/Shutterstock; 109: Burlingham/Shutterstock; 112: Gary Cook/www.cartoonstock.com; 120 (bottom, left): Blackdiamond67/Fotolia; 120 (bottom, right): Dmitry/Fotolia; 120 (top, left): Butterfly photos.org/Fotolia; 120 (top, right): Ron Rowan/Fotolia; 127: Kes/www.cartoonstock.com; 139: B Christopher/Alamy Stock Photo; 140 (bottom): Alexander Khripunov/Fotolia; 140 (top): Ognianmed/Fotolia; 141 (bottom): Bborriss/Fotolia; 141 (top): Elnur/Shutterstock; 143: Wildman/Fotolia; 147: Photo courtesy of David Root; 148: © Randy Glasbergen/glasbergen.com; 167: Peter Hesse/www.cartoonstock.com; 175 (left): Mocker_Bat/Fotolia; 175 (right): Monkey Business Images/Shutterstock; 176 (left): Bombaert Patrick/Alamy Stock Photo; 176 (right): Sunshine Pics/Alamy Stock Photo; 177 (bottom): Stocksnapper/Shutterstock; 177 (top): Stocksnapper/Shutterstock; 191: Monkey Business Images/Shutterstock; 193: Isabella Bannerman/www.cartoonstock.com; 213: Vkarlov/Fotolia; 221: Ramon Berk/Shutterstock; 228: Chris Wildt/www.cartoonstock.com.